BRITISH COMMA
in action

By Leroy Thompson

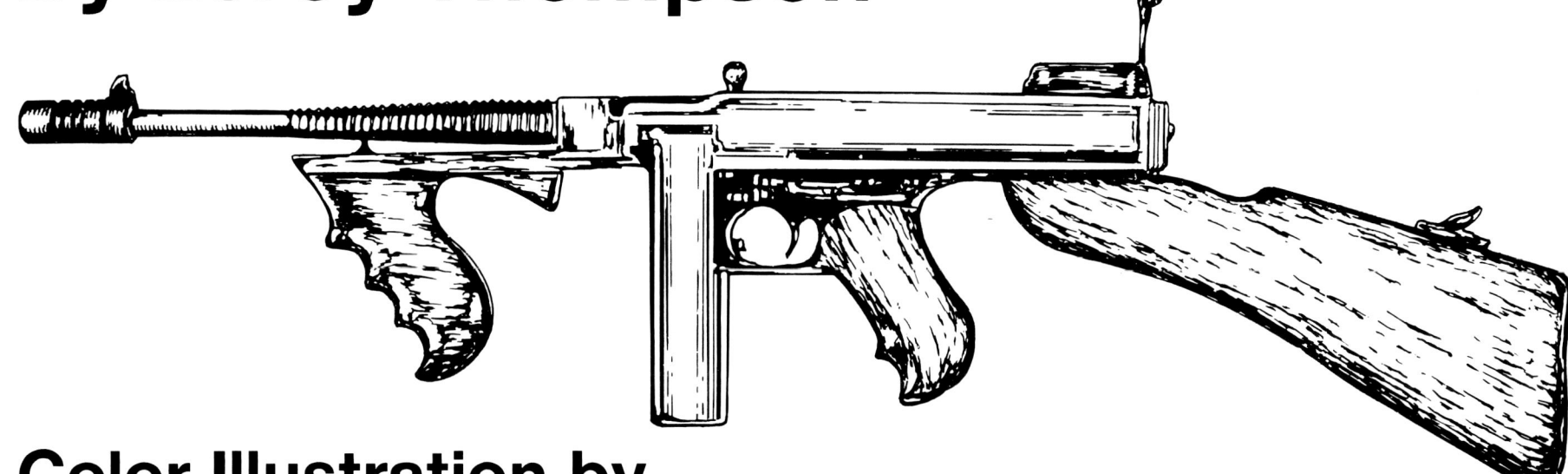

Color Illustration by Ken MacSwan

Illustrated by Joe Sewell

squadron/signal publications, inc.
Combat Troops In Action No.8

(Cover) Members of #3 Commando storm ashore along the coast of France on a raid in force. Commandos became such an emotional problem for the Germans that Hitler ordered captured Commandos to be summarily executed.

COPYRIGHT © 1987 SQUADRON/SIGNAL PUBLICATIONS, INC.
1115 CROWLEY DRIVE   CARROLLTON, TEXAS 75011-5010
All rights reserved. No part of this publication may be reproduced, stored in a retrieval system or transmitted in any form by any means electrical, mechanical or otherwise, without written permission of the publisher.

ISBN 0-89747-192-X

If you have any photographs of the aircraft, armor, soldiers or ships of any nation, particularly wartime snapshots, why not share them with us and help make Squadron/Signal's books all the more interesting and complete in the future. Any photograph sent to us will be copied and the original returned. The donor will be fully credited for any photos used. Please send them to:
Squadron/Signal Publications, Inc., 1115 Crowley Dr., Carrollton, TX 75011-5010.

A German soldier's nightmare. This member of #3 Commando carries his F-S dagger clutched in his teeth. While this method of carrying the dagger may look rather theatrical, it was in fact, not unusual and served to keep the weapon readily available while making a final approach on a sentry when both hands needed to be free. (1941)

From The Independent Companies
To The Special Service Brigade

During the spring of 1940 the so-called Independent Companies were formed to carry out raids against the Germans along the coast of Normandy. These companies were drawn from Territorial Army (TA) units, which were roughly the equivalent of American reserve units, and were intended to be amphibious raiders. Each Independent Company was to have a strength of twenty-one officers and 268 other ranks including engineers, medical personnel, as well as other specialist troops. The ten Independent Companies were formed as follows:

#1 Company - formed April 1940 from the 52nd Lowland Division
#2 Company - formed April 1940 from the 53rd Welch Regiment
#3 Company - formed April 1940 from the 54th East Anglian Division
#4 Company - formed April 1940 from the 55th West Lancashire Division
#5 Company - formed April 1940 from the 56th (1st London) Division
#6 Company - formed April 1940 from the 9th Scottish Division
#7 Company - formed April 1940 from the 15th Scottish Division
#8 Company - formed April 1940 from the 18th Eastern Division
#9 Company - formed April 1940 from the 38th Welch Division
#10 Company - formed April 1940 from the 66th East Lancashire Division

Under LTC Colin Gubbins, who would later become famous as the founder of Special Operations Executive (SOE), the 1st through the 5th Independent Companies were sent to Norway in May of 1940. Designated 'Scissors Force', these companies were charged with preventing the Germans from occupying Bodo, Mo, and Mosjoen, and harassing the German advance. Unfortunately, as has often been the case with elite raiding units, they were misused as conventional infantry, diluting their effectiveness. By late May 'Scissors Force' had been pulled out of Norway. The other five Independent Companies, though they had been aboard ship ready to leave for Norway, had not been sent into action.

After the fall of France and the low countries, and the courageous but humiliating exit of the British Expeditionary Force from Dunkirk in June of 1940, LT COL Dudley Clarke suggested the formation of small lightly armed formations that could conduct guerrilla like operations behind enemy lines. Submitted to Winston Churchill, even the name *Commando*, after the hard hitting *Boer Commandos* of the Boer War in South Africa struck a familiar note in the Prime Minister who had seen the Boer Commandoes in action as a war correspondent during the Boer War. Churchill, envisioning *'...a ceaseless offensive against a whole German occupied coastline, leaving a trail of German corpses behind...'*, pushed for the idea and quickly got Clarke the approval he needed.

Originally, the Commando Companies were to total about 5,000 men. The successes and failures of the South African Boer Commandos were studied in detail — and the decision was made to form units to act as raiders/guerrillas to carry out hit-and-run raids of not more than 48 hours in duration, 'butcher and bolt' along the entire coast of occupied Europe. It was further expected that these Commando units would also carry out certain clandestine missions, with each Commando being composed of some 500 men broken into ten troops of fifty men each.

Initially, the various Army commands were given the responsibility of forming the eleven Commando units:

#1 Commando - from The Independent Companies
#2 Commando - from parachute qualified recruits of all commands, since this unit was envisioned as an airorne commando unit.
#3 Commando - from Southern Command
#4 Commando - from Southern Command
#5 Commando - from Western Command
#6 Commando - from Western Command
#7 Commando - from Eastern Command
#8 Commando - from London and the Household Division
#9 Commando - from Scottish Command
#10 Commando - from Northern Command
#11 Commando - from Scottish Command
#12 Commando - formed later from men stationed in Northern Ireland

To plan Commando operations, MO9 was formed under the Director of Military Operations and Plans. Headed by LT COL Dudley Clarke, this planning command was initially known as Offensive Operations but was soon changed to Combined Operations. Churchill, ever impatient for action, kept pushing for the Commandos to carry out operations *"...at the earliest possible moment"*.

In June of 1940, #11 Independent Company was formed with twenty-five officers and 350 other ranks drawn from the other Independent Companies. Those troops of the Independent Companies not incorporated into this *Commando Unit* were assigned to help defend Britain against what was believed to be the very real possibility of a German invasion of the United Kingdom. Less than two weeks after the formation of #11 Independent Company some of its members carried out the first 'commando' raid near Boulogne on the French Coast where five separate groups landed to probe German defenses. During the approximately eighty minutes spent ashore some of the Commandos did encounter Germans, with whom they exchanged fire, but little of value was accomplished. The fledgling Commandos even forgot to search the bodies of two Germans that were killed.

This raid on occupied France was primarily for morale purposes to demonstrate to the British public that the Army was striking back. Ironically, the only Commando casualty was Dudley Clarke who had gone along as an observer. Fortunately, he was only slightly wounded.

The next raid, code named AMBASSADOR, took place on the night of 14/15 July against the German garrison on Guernsey. Members of #11 Independent Company and #3 Commando carried out the raid, which was unsuccessful due to choosing poor landing sites and the unsuitability of RAF Crash Boats being used as raiding craft. However, the Commandos were quickly learning from their mistakes, making changes in tactics and equipment. On 17 July 1940 Admiral of the Fleet Sir Roger Keyes was named Director of Combined Operations. A close friend of Churchill, Keyes would prove a sound choice since he combined both organizational ability and aggressiveness.

In October of 1940 the various Independent Companies and Commandos were organized into Special Service Battalions (SSB) comprised of two 500-man companies each:

1st Special Service Battalion - based at Dartmouth and Paignton was formed from 1-5 & 8 and 9 Independent Companies.
2nd Special Service Battalion - based at Whitney Bay, Scotland was formed from 6 and 7 Independent Companies & 9 & 11 Commandos
3rd Special Service Battalion - based at Girvan, Scotland was formed from #4 and #7 Commandos
4th Special Service Battalion - based at Largs was formed from #3 and #8 Commandos
5th Special Service Battalion - based at Helensburgh was formed from #5 and #6 Commandos

#2 Commando was the basis for the 1st Parachute Battalion which evolved into the Parachute Regiment. #12 Commando remained independent since it was formed for possible use in Ireland should the Germans invade the Island. #10 Independent Company had been dispatched with the Royal Marines to Dakar but returned to the UK in October of 1940, where it was disbanded with a number of its members joining one of the Special Service Battalions. The five Special Service Battalions formed the Special Service Brigade (SSB) under the command of Brigadier J.C. Haydon.

Russel Miller has pointed out that *"No matter what their nationality or allegiance, units of commando-style troops the world over were employed for the most hazardous of the War's tasks. Almost always their members were volunteers. They were romantic, independent, often fanatical, sometimes eccentric, occasionally suicidal. They all knew beforehand that their capture might mean death before a firing squad. Facing that ultimate possibility required two exceptional characteristics: outstanding courage and an unquenchable lust for war."*

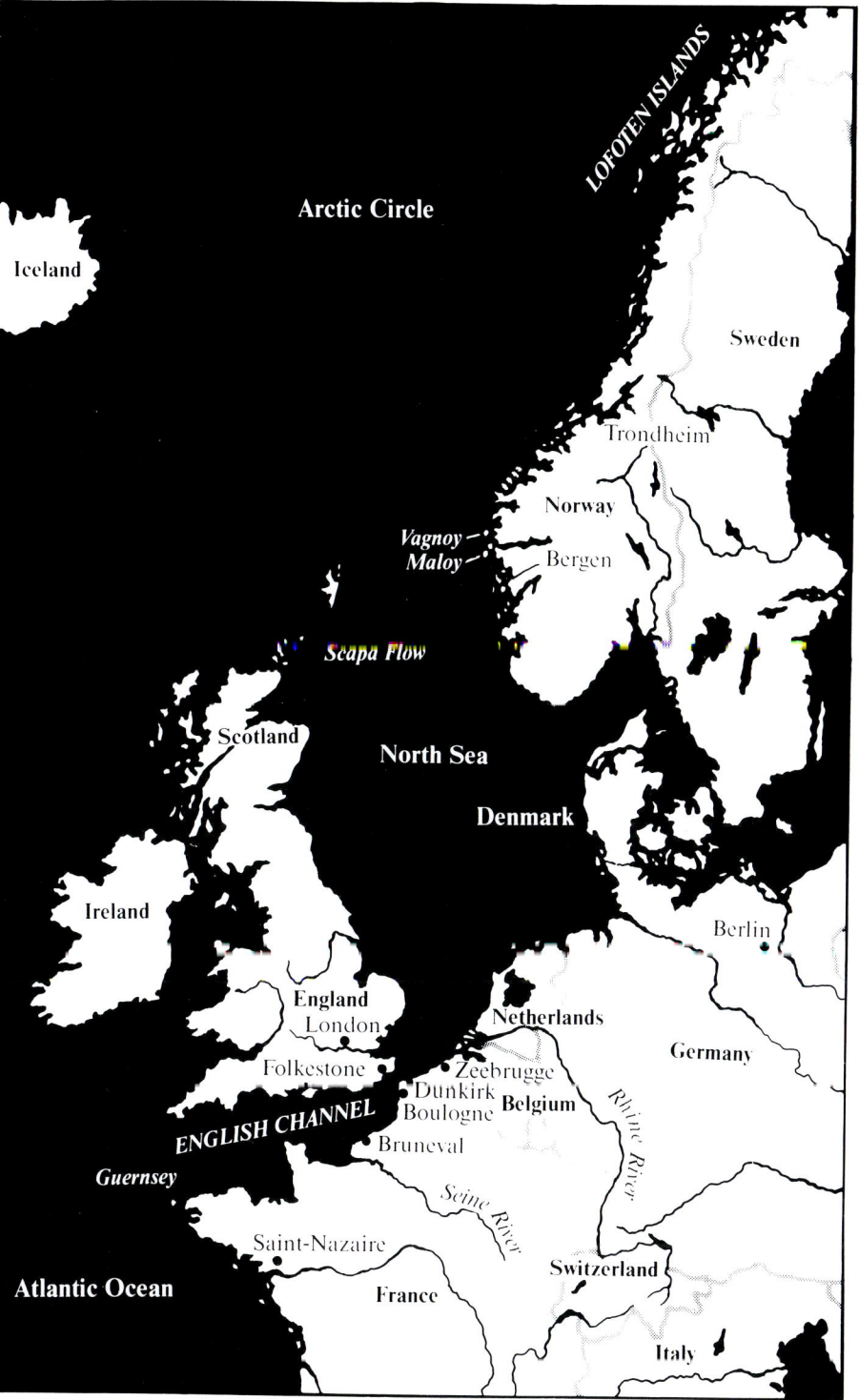

Training

In October of 1940, the Combined Training Center was established at Achnicarry, Scotland to train Commandos for amphibious raids. Initially the Commando training course ran three months, however, later in the war it was shortened to five weeks. Physical conditioning was rigorous, including swimming in full equipment, assault courses with live ammunition, obstacle courses, climbing, and exercises carried out in groups of eight using a heavy log as weight. Training was carried out using the 'buddy system', with two men being necessary to complete many parts of training, especially the obstacle course.

The obstacle course was designed to build self reliance and self confidence. Rather than being billeted in barracks, for example, the Commandos were normally provided with a living allowance and expected to board in the community near the training center. If a commando chose to keep the money and sleep in a field, it was their business as long as they managed to maintain a military demeanor. This system of living independently was part of their training in self-reliance. Another aspect of their training were the formations, which would often be designated to be held at a site a 100 miles or more away — for the next day. It was up to the Commando to be at the formation with his required kit — on time. During training, Commandos were encouraged to make any suggestions which might offer a better way to do something. Unlike most military organizations, the Commandos encouraged initiative.

A specific skill taught during Commando training was demolitions, which included the use of electrical detonators, drilling of bore holes, and placement of explosive charges. Special techniques for destroying railways, machinery, boilers, fuel dumps, and other likely targets were taught.

Commandos at Achnicarry Training Center cross a rope bridge while explosions are set off beneath them. The use of explosives and live ammunition during training was more dangerous for the Commandos but provided them with very realistic training.

Commando trainees learn to use the edge of their helmets to deliver a devastating and usually fatal blow to the neck. Under the tutelage of former Shanghai International Settlement Policemen W.E. Fairbairn and E.A. Sykes, the Commandos received intensive hand-to-hand combat training.

To develop strength Commandos trainees made great use of the log, both tossing it and marching while carrying it. Developing stamina and co-ordination was the purpose of much of the Commando training.

Commandos move through an obstacle course during training to learn both stalking and rapid silent movement. TO BERLIN can be seen written on the board above the crawling Commando. Both are wearing stocking caps/balaclavas.

Full field kit were a normal part of Commando training even during climbing and speed marches. These Commandos undergoing training are armed with the Lee-Enfield rifle.

Commandos learned to use both ends of the rifle, either the bayonet or the butt with equal effectiveness.

Under a pair of tough former Shanghai International Policemen named W.E. Fairbairn and A.E. Sykes, the close combat training was especially practical and demanding, making the Commandos among some of the best close-in fighters in military history. Training included hand-to-hand combat, knife-fighting, use of the bayonet, use of the pistol, use of the Thompson Sub-Machine Gun, use of grenades, assault tactics with both the rifle and Bren gun, and stalking and fighting in urban areas. The famed Fairbairn-Sykes dagger was developed by the instructors and Commandos were taught to use it with quiet and deadly efficiency. Other weapons the Commandos were taught to use for silent killing included the edge of their helmets, the butt of their rifles, piano wire garrotes. Firearms training was much more intense and practical than that given to most military personnel and emphasized rapid target acquisition and decision making. Many of the shooting techniques developed by Fairbairn in Shanghai were incorporated into Commando training, including rooms with mannequin targets dressed in either British or German uniforms. Mock towns through which Commandos would have to pass, engaging pop-up and other types of targets as they appeared.

The assault course included additional special firing ranges but also emphasized other practical skills. Amphibious landings, for example, were stressed as was boat handling and other nautical skills including navigation, the latter proving invaluable on at least one occasion when a Commando navigated a craft back to Britain after a raid when all of the naval personnel aboard had been killed. Clearing obstacles and mines was practiced during obstacle course training as well as bridging, including toggle bridging using toggles and ropes carried by each Commando. The use of assault boats for raiding and the use of scaling ladders was also taught during the obstacle course.

The tactical portion of the Achnicarry course included field survival and land navigation. An important part of field survival was learning to butcher and prepare all types of meat in the field, rendering the Commandos much more self-sufficient than other formations. Land navigation included extensive map reading and recognition of land marks. Small unit tactics concentrated on silent movement, setting up ambushes, immediate re-action drills in case of ambush, night tactics, and setting up road blocks.

Commandos learned to use heavy infantry weapons up to and including 3 inch mortars and anti-tank weapons — early in the war the Boys anti-tank rifle, but later the Piat was used. Commando officers and NCOs were expected to lead by example and to be even better trained than their men. Many NCOs and officers passed through the instructor's course, which lasted an additional two to four weeks and included intensive training in the skills already learned during the basic Commando course so that the instructor could teach these skills to trainees.

(Right) The rugged Scottish terrain offered an excellent training ground for Commandos to learn rock climbing, rapelling, and survival training in general.

(Below) Armed with a Thompson SMG this Commando free climbs a cliff in Scotland. During training the Thompson usually had no magazine.

The ability to survive in the field could be of over-riding importance for Commandos so field butchery of both wild and domestic animals was taught.

During assault courses the Commandos learned to overcome any fear of barriers. This Commando throws himself on a barbwire fence so those following him can run over his body to rapidly clear the barrier.

Commandos learned to combine climbing and stalking skills in order to set an ambush position in a tree. Toggle ropes for crossing ravines or rivers can be seen attached to this rather well used tree.

The following Bren gunner clears the barbwire barrier by running across the body of his comrade. Cloth covers are worn over the Mk I helmets.

Members of #3 Commando learning judo, in this case the major hip toss. Hand to hand combat was stressed in Commando training making the Commandos rather dangerous to the enemy in the field.

Commandos learned to quickly disarm an enemy with a rifle. The dents in the top of the helmet of the instructor, no doubt offer an interesting story, since instructors were usually combat veterans.

A #3 Commando trainee learns to kill an enemy sentry using a choke hold. Both are wearing the British Mark I helmet, the shape of which made it a lethal weapon in the hands of a trained Commando.

Commandos being issued equipment prior to receiving ski training. Dress codes were not enforced quite as rigorously among Commandoes as it was among regular army troops, hence the disparity in headgear such as berets, field service caps, and Glengarries, which are all being worn.

Cross country skiing was one of the more important survival techniques for Commandos, especially those anticipating raids into Norway during the long winter months.

An instructor illustrates the technique for hitting a prone firing position while remaining on skis.

A Commando undergoing stalking training in a swampy area such as found along the coasts of Northern Europe. Training was usually conducted in the most realistic terrain available.

The armored landing craft allowed Commandos to remain safe from small arms fire until the front gate was lowered and they stormed out into the water.

Being able to rapidly exit an assault craft could sometimes mean the difference between life and death, or success and failure of a raid.

This Free French Army Commando of #10 (IA) Commando demonstrates how to deliver a killing thrust to the carotid artery with the F-S dagger. The F-S dagger became symbolic of the Commando.

First pattern F-S daggers are being passed out to members of #3 Commando. This was a big day in the life of a Commando.

A French Naval Infantry Commando serving with the British sharpens his F-S dagger. He wears the striped long sleeve naval t-shirt and Naval Infantry Commando beret badge which mark him as being a French Commando.

During training a Commando learns to quickly incapacitate a German sentry. Training was often conducted with adversaries in full German uniform in order to acclimate the trainee to the enemy.

Sharpening their F-S daggers was a favorite relaxation for Commandos as these French Naval Infantry Commandos of #10 (IA) Commando are doing.

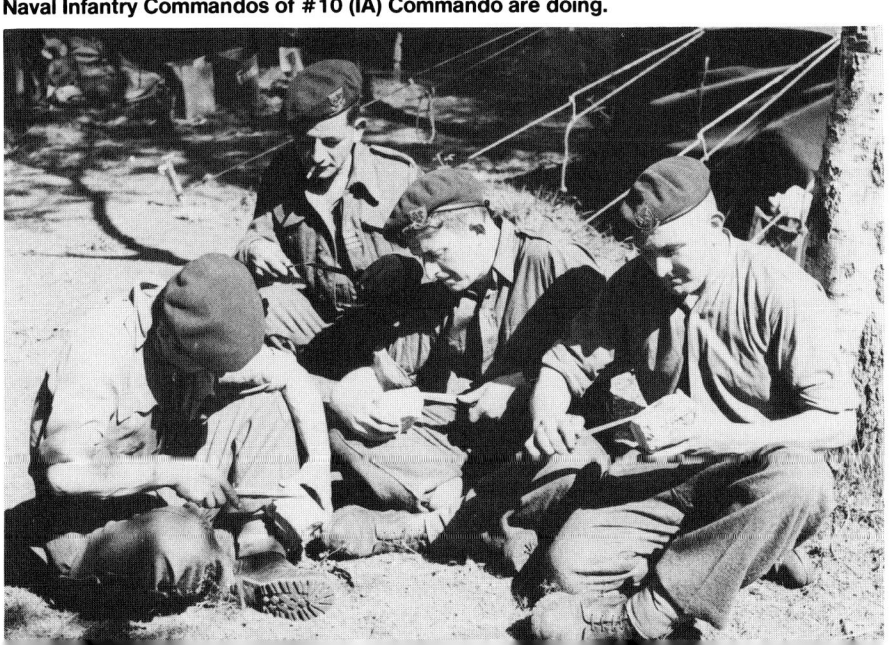

Fairbairn-Sykes Dagger (1st Pattern)

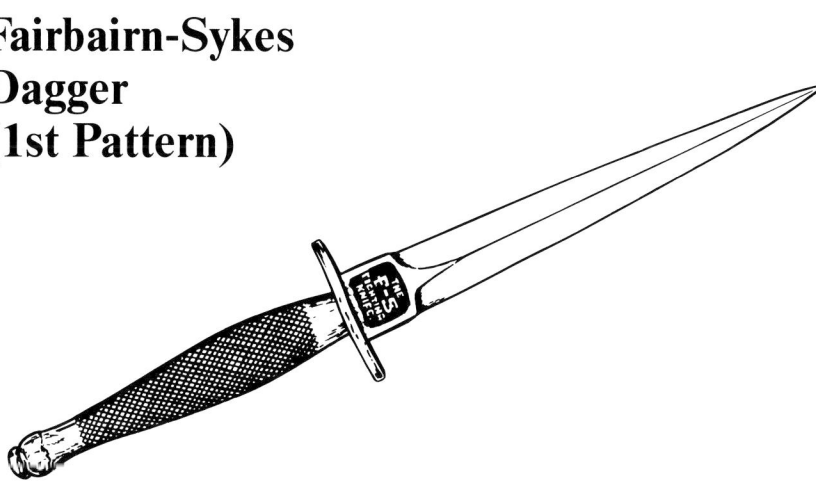

13

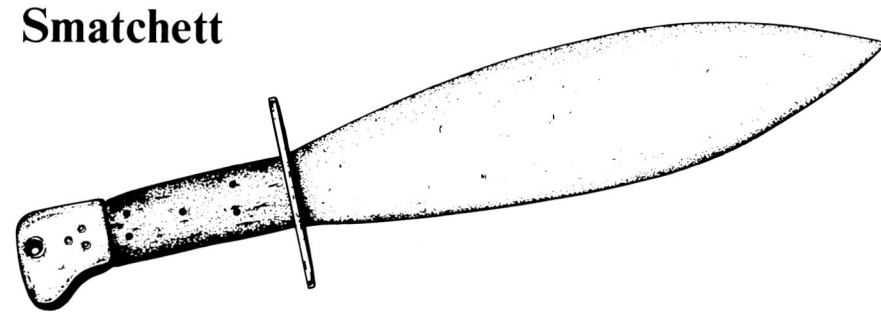

(Above) This French Commando wears his balaclava, possibly so that he would not be recognized should his photograph appear in the press and possibly end up in German hands.

Smatchett

(Left) Although the Commandos' most famous weapon was the F-S dagger, the Smatchett was also used and was a formidable close quarters weapon.

French Naval Infantry Commando of #10 (IA) Commando wears a Junior Lieutenant's insignia, France, No 10 Commando arcs, and a round Combined Operations patch on his shoulder and sleeve.

A French Commando stops for water during a speed march with full field pack. Marches like these quickly increased the stamina of a Commando.

French Commandos carry out a speed march wearing the French M1915 helmets. Wearing helmets or other pieces of their national uniforms was a matter of great pride among foreign nationals recruited into the Commandos.

Free French Army Commandos undergoing an inspection, wear the Cross of Lorraine beret badge, which differs markedly from the Naval Infantry cap badge worn by other French Commandos.

Commando engineers carried a specialized pack board on which they mounted their sapper equipment.

French Commandos learn to handle and land from dories at Achnicarry in August of 1943.

A pair of Commandos of 101 Troop of #6 Commando bring their kayak ashore. The man in the foreground is lifting a Bren Gun out of the two man boat.

Raids in Norway
The Lofoten Isalands And Vaagso

In the largest raid so far in the war, 500 commandos of #3 and #4 Special Service Battalions, a detachment of Royal Engineers, and 52 Norwegian volunteers carried out a raid on the Lofoten Islands, the heart of the Norwegian fish oil industry, on 4 March 1941. Located off the coast of Northern Norway, these islands were of little strategic significance, however, they had a small German garrison and were an easily accessible target on the sea. The raid was highly successful with the Commandos destroying German military installations and eighteen fish oil factories. More than 800,000 gallons of oil and fuel were destroyed, and eleven small ships were sunk totaling 20,000 tons. However, the raid's greatest contribution was toward morale at home, 225 Germans and sixty 'Quislings' (Norwegian turncoats) were taken prisoner. As an additional *"tug on Hitler's mustache"*, the Commandos sent a telegram to *A. Hitler*, Berlin letting him know they were there.

315 Norwegians hoping to join the Free Norwegian forces, or just wishing to escape the Nazi occupation, returned to England with the Commandos. Even though their livelihood had been severely damaged the local Norwegian townspeople gathered on the dock to sing the Norwegian national anthem and cheer as the British ships left the harbor.

Perhaps the most important accomplishment other than building morale and showing the Germans that their European conquests were not entirely secure was the capture by the Commandos of a set of extra rotors for an *Enigma* machine from a German ship in the harbor. Further, the destruction of the fish oil factories actually had more strategic impact than might be originally supposed, since fish oil was used in manufacturing nitro-glycerine. During the hours the Commandos were ashore their only casualty was an officer who managed to shoot himself in his own foot.

Even before the Lofoten raid the decision had been made to redesignate the Special Service Battalions back to Commandos and by mid-March of 1941, this process was completed as follows:

#1 Commando - based at Dartmouth from 1 Special Service Battalion
#2 Commando - based at Weymouth from 1 Special Service Battalion
#3 Commando - based at Largs from 4 Special Service Battalion
#4 Commando - based at Troon from 3 Special Service Battalion
#5 Commando - based at Falmouth from 5 Special Service Battalion
#6 Commando - based at Inveraray from 5 Special Service Battalion
#7 Commando - based in the Middle East from 3 Special Service Battalion
#8 Commando - based in the Middle East from 4 Special Service Battalion
#9 Commando - based at Criccieth from 2 Special Service Battalion
#11 Commando - based in the Middle East from 2 Special Service Battalion
#12 Commando - based at Warsash had remained separate from the Special Service Brigade

The men of the Commandos were pleased with this change since they had never felt the same loyalty to the Special Service Battalions that they had to their Commando. Not long after this redesignation 1, 2, 4, 6, 9, and 12 Commandos were earmarked to help seize the Canary Islands if Spain entered the war on the side of Germany. As it turned out this operation was unnecessary, but the Canary Islands contingency plan tied down a large number of Commandos. And during the Autumn of 1941, some one hundred Commandos were detached from various Commandos for a possible operation in West Africa, but this operation too was eventually cancelled in February of 1942.

A small detachment of Commandos involved a small group detached to Special Operations Executive (SOE) late in 1940. Using a fishing trawler named Maid Honour,

Wearing tams, a group of Commandos study a sand table model of an objective along the French coast prior to a raid. Meticulously detailed planning like this helped to make the raids successful and keep commando raiders alive.

this group was earmarked to carry out clandestine cross-channel operations out of Poole, Dorset (the present training site of the Special Boat Squadron, the elite combat swimmers of today's Royal Marine Commandos). During late 1941 Maid Honour was used to check the West African coast for U-boat bases, and in July of 1942 the trawler was involved in secretly hi-jacking Italian and German ships from the Spanish Island of Fernando Po. In July of 1942 the Maid was taken out of SOE service.

The first half of 1941, with the exception of the raid on the Lofoten Islands, saw only limited small scale reconnaissance raids carried out by the Commandos against the French Coast. A shortage of landing craft was a contributing factor to limiting the scale of raids. Still, even these small raids raised morale of the British public and they pointed up the German's vulnerability. These Commando raids forced the Wehrmacht to tie down increasingly large numbers of men on coastal garrison duty. On 27 October 1941, in one of the most important moves for the Commandos, Lord Louis Mountbatten, cousin to the King, was appointed the Chief of Combined Operations.

The Commandos blacken each other's faces and receive a final briefing before landing.

Besides destroying 800,000 gallons of fish oil at Lofoten Island, Commandos destroyed 20,000 tons of shipping and brought back 225 German prisoners.

Commandos board ship for a cross channel raid against a target on the French coast.

Commandos setting out on a motor launch at dusk for a raid on the French coast. Leaving at about dusk will put the raiders along the French coast well into the night.

Lord Lovat (tall officer at center right facing the others) talks to his Commandos prior to a raid. The Fairbairn-Sykes (F-S) Commando dagger is worn on the leg of the Commando in the right foreground.

This Member of #3 Commando wears a Brown Drab burlap cover over his steel helmet. (c. 1941)

This Member of #3 Commando is armed with an M1 Thompson Sub Machine Gun. The hard hitting .45 caliber Thompson was a favorite among the Commandos.

(Above) In addition to the Combined Operations insignia, this Commando wears a pair of parachute wings, commando arc and also wears the badge of his former regiment upon his Green beret. (c. 1941)

"Outstanding Courage, and An Unquenchable Lust For War"

A member of #3 Commando blackens the face of a seated Commando holding a Bren Gun magazine. A pair of wire cutters and a toggle rope are carried at the waist of the 'make up artist'. (IWM)

Commandos aboard ship after the Lofoton Islands raid in March of 1941. While carried on early raids the Thompson SMG was in very short supply, being drawn from the armoury for a raid and returned afterwards.

Members of 101 Troop of #6 Commando; this troop specialized in small boat operations and was a forerunner of the SBS. The officer in the lead carries a long barreled artillery Luger with a snail drum magazine in place!

Vaagso

Very late in 1941, only weeks after Mountbatten assumed command, the Commandos mounted their largest operation so far of the war — again in Norway. On 26 December, 300 men from #12 Commando again landed in the Lofoten Islands, but this time it was a diversion for a larger operation much further south at Vaagso on the Norwegian coast just south of Trondheim. Unlike Lofoten, Vaasgo was heavily fortified with coastal batteries and defended by German garrisons. Carried out under the code name OPERATION ARCHERY by members of #2 and #3 Commando plus a contingent of Royal Engineers from #6 Commando under the leadership of COL John Dunford-Slater, who had led the LOFOTEN Islands raid earlier in the year, this would be a true joint service operation with the Royal Navy and Royal Air Force.

Early on the morning of 27 December as the raiding force silently sailed into the fjord a German lookout spotted them, but his repeated telephone calls were met with disbelief and accusations of drunkenness. Only one minute behind schedule the landing craft were lowered into the water. All question of the origin of the ships was dispelled when a salvo of six inch shells from the Cruiser KENYA came crashing into the German batteries on Maloy at 8:48 a.m. followed two minutes later by shells from four destroyers. Shells were coming in at the rate of fifty per minute destroying the barracks and three of the four guns. Under this covering fire landing craft full of Commandos approached the island. As the Commandos landed the naval fire was lifted and Hampden bombers swooped in dropping smoke bombs. Despite their surprise the Germans put up fierce resistance, with the Commandos having to fight house to house to secure the Island. By 10:20 the reserves had to be committed.

At 3:00 pm, as the arctic sun was setting, the Commandos were back aboard ship with seventy-one Norwegian volunteers and 150 German prisoners. They had suffered nineteen dead, fifty-two wounded and killed 150 Germans. Despite their losses, the overall raid was a resounding success, the Destroyers sank nine merchant ships and an armed German trawler was captured, along with the ship's secret code books which provided invaluable intelligence.

Mountbatten viewed this raid as a 'test run' for larger joint service raids in the future. Commando leaders made it a point to lead from the front and often adopted 'eccentric' aids for their men to locate them in battle. "Mad Jack" Churchill, the 2nd in command of #3 Commando, led Troops 5 and 6 ashore playing his bagpipes. One of the most tangible results of the Vaagso raid and the occupation of the Lofoten Islands for two days as part of the operation was that 30,000 additional German troops were sent to Norway to garrison coastal areas against further Commando raids. A few hundred Commandos proved to be very cost effective.

(Above) A #3 Commando trooper places his F-S dagger in its sheath, which has been strapped to his calf. A second knife was sometimes carried in this position. The steel helmet is covered by a net instead of a burlap cover.

Fairbairn-Sykes Dagger (2nd Pattern)

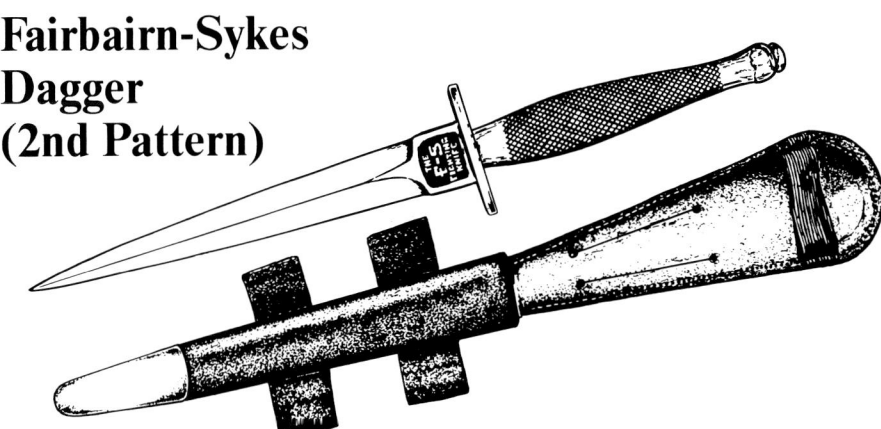

(Left) Commandos back aboard ship after the Vaagso raid in December of 1941, display the Union Jack they carried with them.

St Nazaire And Madagascar

Early in 1942 command of the Special Service Brigade passed to R.H. Laycock. The new year also saw plans progressing for the commando's most famous raid, OPERATION CHARIOT, the raid on the drydock at St. Nazaire. The only drydock on the French Atlantic Coast capable of handling capital ships, was selected as a target in early 1942 in order to deny the Tirpitz a base on the Atlantic. Plans called for the destruction of the drydock and damaging the nearby U-Boat pens.

The final plan called for the destroyer H.M.S. CAMPBELLTOWN to ram the drydock gates, after which demolition charges would be placed. The destroyer itself was to be filled with explosives using a delayed fuse. #2 Commando provided the primary assault force, while demolition parties were formed of volunteers from #1, 3, 4, 5, 9, and 12 Commandos. Dress rehearsals for the raid were held at Devonport dockyard.

On the evening of 27 March Commandos aboard motor launches approached the French Coast. Some of these launches were hit by gunfire and a number of Commandos were killed. The destroyer CAMPBELLTOWN also took heavy casualties during its approach, but rammed the drydock gates at 01:34 on the morning of the 28th. In support of the raid an RAF attack was launched simultaneously. As soon as the CAMPBELLTOWN rammed the drydock gates demolition parties set their charges, while Commando assault parties hit German gun emplacements. Once the charges were set off the Commandos and crew of the destroyer began to retreat to the motor launches under heavy fire. Unfortunately, during the approach and assault many of the motor launches had been destroyed, forcing many of the Commandos to take to the countryside. When LT COL Newman told his men to fight their way out of the docks and break into the countryside, his orders were met with grins from men delighted to carry on the 'scrap'. Most were later taken prisoner. Only five managed to evade capture and return to England with the help of the French Resistance.

During OPERATION CHARIOT the Royal Navy lost 85 killed and 106 captured, and of the 241 Commandos involved 59 were killed or missing and 109 were captured. Five Victoria Crosses were awarded to participants of the operation. The delayed charges in CAMPBELLTOWN caused even greater destruction when the explosives went off since the Germans had not noticed their presence.

Because of the success of CHARIOT a similar raid was planned under the code OPERATION FOXROCK for June of 1942. One hundred members of #12 Commando were to destroy lockgates and other installations at St. Valery-en-Caux, but the operation was aborted when German aircraft spotted the assault force crossing the Channel. OPERATION ABERCROMBY had to be aborted in April when 100 men from #4 Commando and fifty Canadians under the command of Lord Lovat attempted a raid on Hardelot village using the new Landing Craft Support (LCS). As it turned out the party landed and re-embarked without doing much damage.

An idea for an operation using Commandos had been germinating since December of 1941 when Winston Churchill had suggested seizing Madagascar from Vichy France as a possible naval base after the fall of Singapore. Plans for seizing Madagascar were drawn up in March of 1942 under the codename IRONCLAD. #5 Commando was designated as part of the assault force and sailed on 23 March, arriving in Durban, South Africa on 22 April 1942.

During IRONCLAD landings on Madagascar, scheduled for 5 May of 1942, #5 Commando's mission was to land a few hours ahead of the main assault force and silence two artillery batteries, which the Commandos did successfully, gaining complete surprise and taking some 300 prisoners. After the main landings the Commandos assisted in capturing the port of Diego Suarez. However, before the entire island could be seized additional amphibious landings proved necessary. Some of the Commandos were used to carry out feints to cover these landings. Other Commandos helped capture the port of Tananrive. Some even acquired horses and formed a 'Commando Cavalry'

during the operation. By early November of 1942, when the French finally surrendered on Madagascar #5 Commando had returned to Great Britain to prepare for other operations.

Early in 1942 it was decided to form a Commando from men of various occupied countries. The Free Dutch had already begun forming a Commando Troop which began going through training at Achnacarry in April of 1942, but the entire Commando did not officially come into existence until June of 1942, when #10 (Inter Allied) Commando was formed and based at Harlech. A British officer, LTC Lister commanded #10 (IA) Commando with individual Commando Troops being commanded by officers from their own countries. Each Commando Troop had an authorized strength of four officers and eighty-three other ranks. Troops were broken down by nationality as follows:

- #1 Troop - French
- #2 Troop - Dutch
- #3 Troop - Miscellaneous nationalities including Austrian, German, Czech, Hungarian, Russian, Rumanian, & other refugees, all of which spoke fluent German.
- #4 Troop - Belgian
- #5 Troop - Norwegian
- #6 Troop - Polish
- #7 Troop - Yugoslavian
- #8 Troop - French
- #9 Troop - Belgian
- #10 Troop - Belgian

The various languages and rank insignias made for a certain amount of confusion in #10 (IA) Commando, but the members of the unit were highly motivated and their national origins was very useful in certain situations.

Commando Beret

Commando Bush Hat

Members of #5 Commando interrogate a French prisoner on Madagascar in May of 1942. The Commando at right wears a 'bush hat' and cut off trousers. (IWM)

An NCO of #5 Commando directs Bren gun fire with his Kukri knife rather than a more traditional Commando edged weapon such as the F-S dagger.

Bren Gun

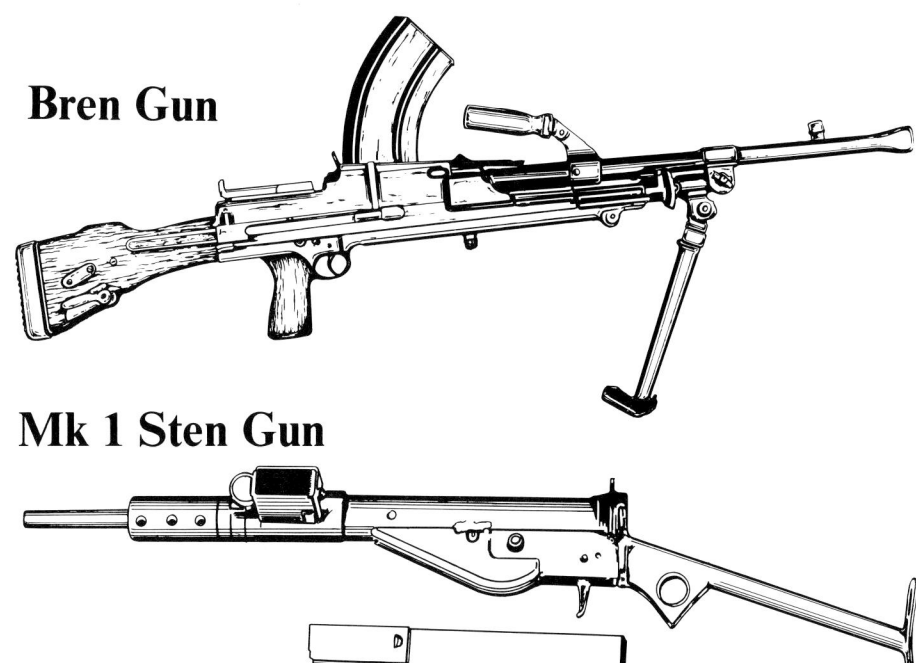

Mk 1 Sten Gun

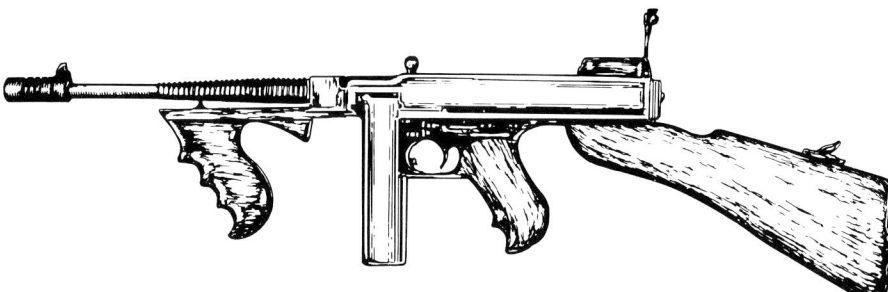

Thompson Submachine Gun Model 1921

Thompson Submachine Gun Model 1928 A1

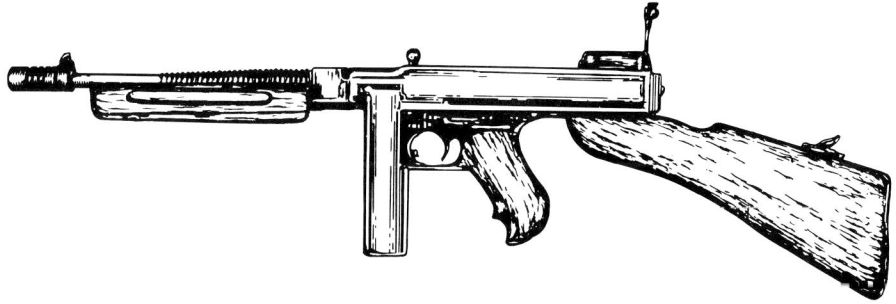

Dieppe

During the late summer of 1942 a major raid was planned against the French coast to test the feasibility of a large-scale opposed landing in France. Dieppe was picked as the test site. #3, #4, and the Royal Marine Commandos were chosen, along with some Canadian infantry battalions, and a Canadian tank battalion as the raiding force. Unfortunately the Germans learned of the raid in advance through traitors in the French resistance and planted the information that there were far fewer defenders at Dieppe than there were. This disinformation was accepted by British intelligence resulting in a gross underestimation of the defenses at Dieppe. The Commandos drew their usual mission of silencing various artillery batteries prior to the landing of infantry and armor. Accompanying the Commandos were a French troop from #10 Commando and fifty American Rangers getting their baptism of fire.

The assault force arrived off Dieppe early on the morning of 19 August coming under heavy fire from shore batteries. Only twenty-five percent of #3 Commando's landing craft were able to reach the correct beach, preventing them from silencing their assigned batteries.

The Royal Marine Commandos were to reinforce the Canadians, but their landing craft were hit while still well off shore preventing them from landing.

Only #4 Commando under Lord Lovat successfully completed its mission, silencing their assigned guns.

Losses were very heavy during the Dieppe landings both among the Commandos and the Canadians who were chewed up on the beaches. Even so valuable lessons were learned about large-scale amphibious assaults.

Beginning in August of 1942 the Small Scale Raiding Force (formerly the Maid Honour Force) began carrying out operations using an MTB (Motor Torpedo Boat). Using the name #62 Commando as a cover, the SSRF was operated directly under Lord Mountbatten for special high priority raids and intelligence gathering missions. At one point the SSRF was being groomed for a raid on the battleship Tirpitz, but this raid was cancelled when the battleship was moved. The SSRF took part in the Dieppe operation in August. In September the SSRF carried out three operations including an attack on a lighthouse in the Channel Islands. These raids usually involved only a dozen or so men and were hit-and-run affairs. While the SSRF was a very small unit it attracted some of the most famous elite forces types including Geoffrey Appleyard and Anders Lassen. Lassen was a Dane who would win both fame and a VC later in the war while with the SBS.

At least partially as a result of SSRF activities, on 18 October 1942 Hitler issued his famous *Commando Order* in which he ordered captured Commandos to be executed. October also saw the expansion of the SSRF to four troops and six Coastal Motor Boats (CMBs) were added to provide the SSRF with more sealift. The expansion of the SSRF brought a new commander, with Bill Stirling (brother of David Stirling who founded the Special Air Service (SAS) in North Africa) taking over.

The major operation involving Commandos in late 1942 was OPERATION TORCH, the Allied landings in North Africa. #1 and #6 Commandos took part in the landings at Algiers along with Americans from the 168th Regimental Combat Team. On the night of 7/8 November 1942 half of #1 Commando captured a fort ten miles west of Algiers and then the airfield at Blida. #6 Commando was not as successful, however, their mission had been to capture another fort on the Bay of Algiers, but landing problems forced them to wait until an airstrike had reduced the fort before they could secure it. The other half of #1 Commando also ran into problems capturing a fort on the Bay of Algiers, when both a naval bombardment and an airstrike was needed before the fort fell.

Also taking part in OPERATION TORCH was #30 Commando, a special intelligence gathering unit, which in addition to normal Commando training had received training

Commandos check their weapons before leaving on the Dieppe raid in August of 1942. A toggle rope is worn by the man checking the bore of his Lee-Enfield rifle. War-time censors have scratched the number designation on the Commando arc of the man at right.

in enemy mines and booby traps, enemy uniforms, equipment and orders of battle, safe cracking, photography, enemy documents, etc. Language skills were a requirement for members of #30 Commando. Each of the Commando's three troops was drawn from a different branch, with #33 Troop from the Royal Marines, #34 Troop from the Army, and #35 Troop from the Royal Navy. #35 Troop was specifically charged with technical intelligence. #30 Commando's mission at Algiers was somewhat optimistic since they were charged with seizing secret documents at the Vichy French Admiralty as well as capturing Admiral Darlan.

In November of 1942 #9 Commando was deployed to Gibraltar against the possibility of an Axis move against the key British base. November also saw the formation of #14 Commando specifically for raids against Norway to insure that German troops continued being heavily garrisoned there. Members of this Commando were specially trained in skiing and cold weather operations. Norwegians from #10 Commando as well as a number of Canadians were assigned to this unit.

Commandos and sailors load men and equipment aboard ship for the Dieppe raid. The Commando at left wears a Free French patch on his shoulder.

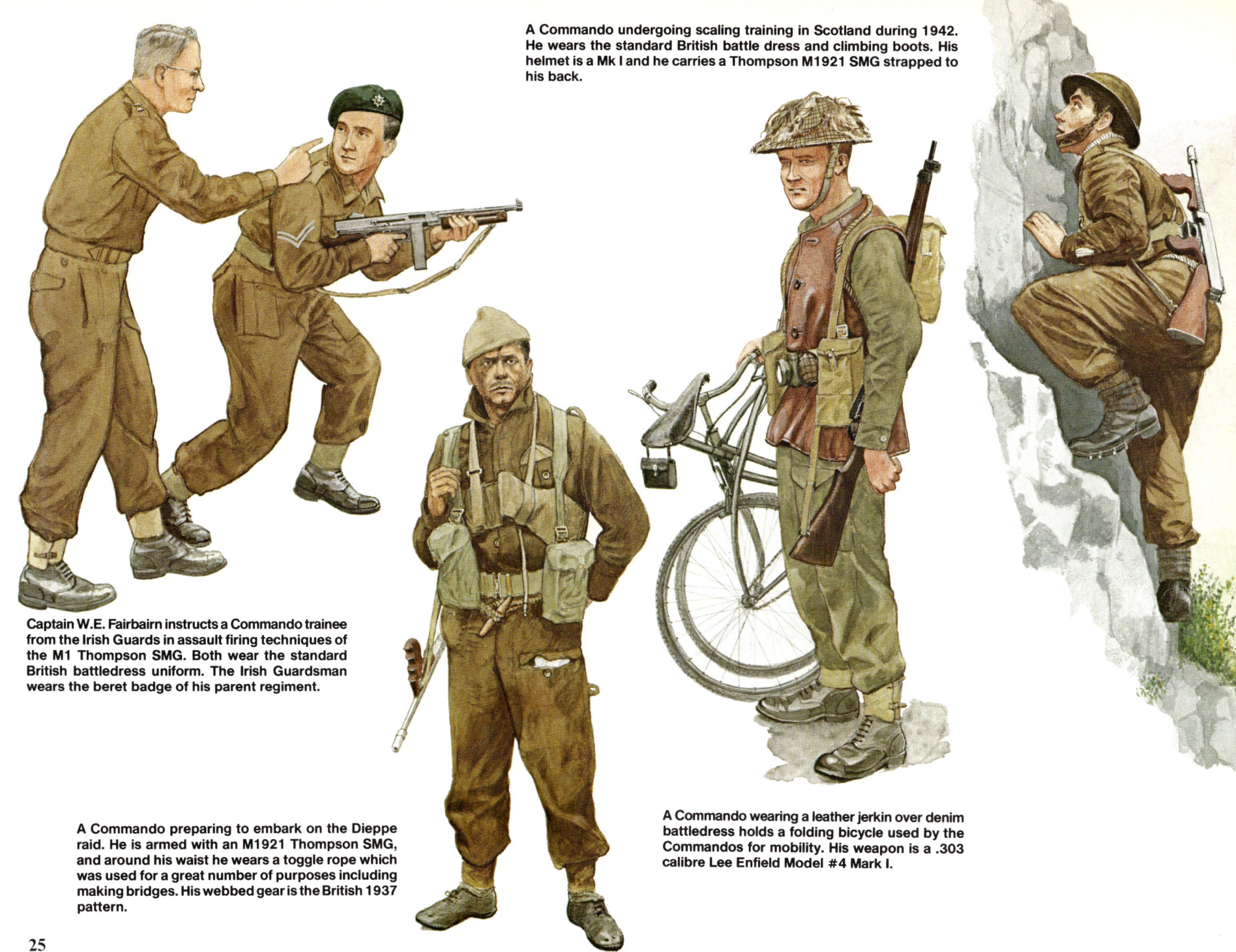

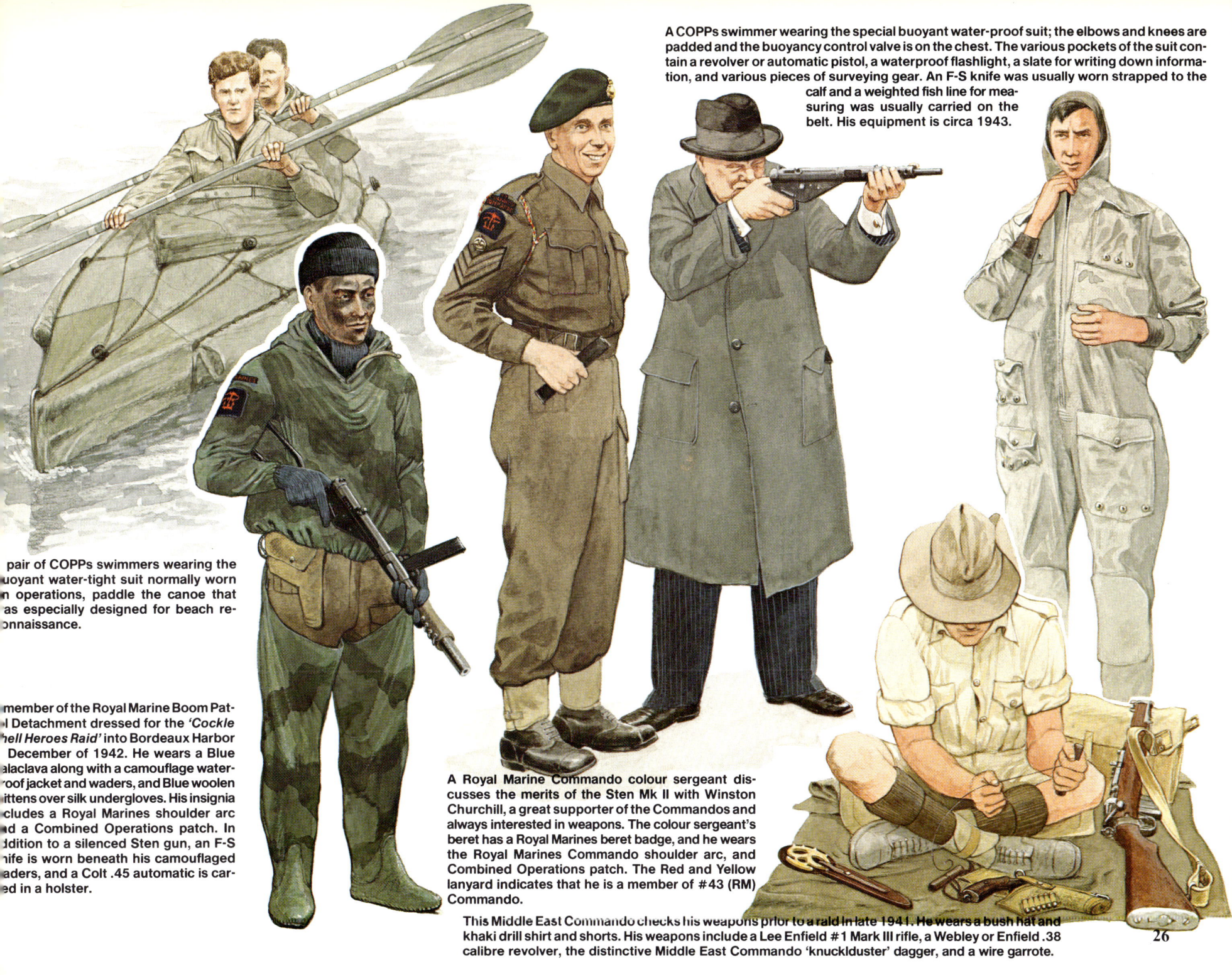

A COPPs swimmer wearing the special buoyant water-proof suit; the elbows and knees are padded and the buoyancy control valve is on the chest. The various pockets of the suit contain a revolver or automatic pistol, a waterproof flashlight, a slate for writing down information, and various pieces of surveying gear. An F-S knife was usually worn strapped to the calf and a weighted fish line for measuring was usually carried on the belt. His equipment is circa 1943.

A pair of COPPs swimmers wearing the buoyant water-tight suit normally worn on operations, paddle the canoe that was especially designed for beach reconnaissance.

A member of the Royal Marine Boom Patrol Detachment dressed for the *'Cockle Shell Heroes Raid'* into Bordeaux Harbor in December of 1942. He wears a Blue balaclava along with a camouflage waterproof jacket and waders, and Blue woolen mittens over silk undergloves. His insignia includes a Royal Marines shoulder arc and a Combined Operations patch. In addition to a silenced Sten gun, an F-S knife is worn beneath his camouflaged waders, and a Colt .45 automatic is carried in a holster.

A Royal Marine Commando colour sergeant discusses the merits of the Sten Mk II with Winston Churchill, a great supporter of the Commandos and always interested in weapons. The colour sergeant's beret has a Royal Marines beret badge, and he wears the Royal Marines Commando shoulder arc, and Combined Operations patch. The Red and Yellow lanyard indicates that he is a member of #43 (RM) Commando.

This Middle East Commando checks his weapons prior to a raid in late 1941. He wears a bush hat and khaki drill shirt and shorts. His weapons include a Lee Enfield #1 Mark III rifle, a Webley or Enfield .38 calibre revolver, the distinctive Middle East Commando 'knuckleduster' dagger, and a wire garrote.

A small motor launch loaded with Commandos on their way to Dieppe. Commandos used a large number of boats this size in a variety of roles.

Returning from Dieppe a wounded Commando is helped from the boat. Casualties among Commandos at Dieppe were very heavy.

All dog-tired, and some wounded after the Dieppe raid, Commandos proudly march off their ships still wearing their stocking caps and blackened faces.

Commandos believed to be of #9 Commando are climbing 'The Rock' when they were sent to reinforce the Gibraltar garrison against a possible Axis move in 1942.

Commandos on Malta examining the trusty Thompson SMG. Malta was bombed continuously but but never invaded, however, fighting an Axis invasion might have been a welcome relief to the Commando's rigorous and continuous training.

A two man canoe could be extremely effective in landing agents in sheltered waters or in moving up small rivers. Getting out of a canoe in mid-water without turning it over was nearly an art.

Commandos practice handling a small boat in a harbor on Malta. Small boats such as these were often used to silently land from motor launches. The three men in the front of the boat are armed with Thompsons, providing a tremendous amount of fire power for such a small craft.

Commandos became extremely adept a crossing obstacles on a rope bridge. The lead Commando carries his trusty Thompson strapped to his back.

Middle East Commando And Layforce

In July of 1940 GHQ Middle Eastern Land Force received a directive from the War Office to form Commando units for raiding purposes. Almost immediately LT COL George Young was ordered to form the first such unit — #50 Middle East (ME) Commando — from forces already in the theater. Among the troops incorporated into #50 ME Commando were some seventy Spaniards, veterans of the Spanish Civil War, who hoped to gain British citizenship by serving in the British Army. In October of 1941 #51 ME Commando was formed by LT COL H.J. Cator from a nucleus of Palestinian Arabs and Jews. Finally, in November of 1941 #52 ME Commando was formed from British volunteers. Additional Commandos were to have been sent to the Mediterranean in October of 1940 to seize Pantellaria, but the operation was cancelled.

Commandos in the Middle East learned the same skills as their counterparts in Europe but with additions such as camel riding, survival on limited water, and forced marches in the desert. Middle East Commandos had difficulty training in amphibious landings due to a shortage of landing craft. All three Middle East Commandos were based at Geneifa. Middle East Commandos adopted their own distinctive headgear and dagger, but instead of a Green beret and F-S dagger they chose a bush hat and a knuckleduster knife.

The first of the Middle East Commandos to see action was #50 ME Commando which was selected for a raid on the Italian seaplane base at Bomba on the night of 27/28 October 1940. The Italian invasion of Greece, however, caused the cancellation of this operation. On 25 November #50 ME Commando was ordered to Crete to aid in the defense of the island. #51 ME Commando also saw its first operation cancelled when a raid against an important water pipeline in North Africa was called off in December of 1940. That same month #52 ME Commando was ordered to the Sudan to aid in its defense. So far the employment of the Middle East Commandos had not been particularly auspicious.

Finally, in January of 1941, #52 ME Commando had the distinction of carrying out the first major raid when they set an ambush behind the Italian lines to cut a main communication road. The raid was not overly successful, however, like many Commando operations it had the residual benefit of tying down large numbers Italian troops in the fear of a repeat performance. Later in January #51 ME Commando arrived in the Sudan and #52 ME Commando returned to Egypt.

In February of 1941, #51 ME Commando carried out important reconnaissance missions for the 4th Indian Division, capturing water holes ahead of their advance. While operating ahead of the 4th Indian Division #51 ME Commando had numerous brushes with Italian troops until their constant harassment convinced the Italians they were facing a much larger force resulting in an Italian withdrawal. #51 ME Commando's adventures continued in May when they played a key role in the capture of the stronghold of Amba Alagi in Ethiopia. Following this operation #51 ME Commando helped Orde Wingate (later to command the Chindits) organize Abyssinian irregulars into an effective fighting force.

While #51 ME Commando was involved in North Africa, #50 ME Commando began operations in the Dodecanese during January of 1941. While operations of #50 Commando continued until March, they were for the most part, abortive due to poor planning on the part of the Royal Navy. As a result #50 ME Commando returned to Egypt in March.

While the three Middle East (ME) Commandos were being formed, plans for sending trained Commando units from the UK to the Mediterranean continued. Planned operations for using UK trained commandos included the capture of Rhodes. Force Z — formed of 7, 8, and 11 Commandos — under the command of LT COL R.E. Laycock was dispatched to the Middle East on 31 January 1941. Arriving at Suez on 7 March, Force Z was redesignated 'Layforce' in order to hide the fact it was a Commando formation. By 10 March Layforce was at Geneifa where #50 and #52 ME Commandos were incorporated into Layforce.

Members of #9 Commando after carrying out a raid on the Garigliano River Estuary in December of 1943 display one of their trophies, a German prisoner. Some of the Commandos appear to be wearing the leather jerkin that became very popular with the Commandos.

Middle East (ME) Commando Dagger (Knuckle Knife)

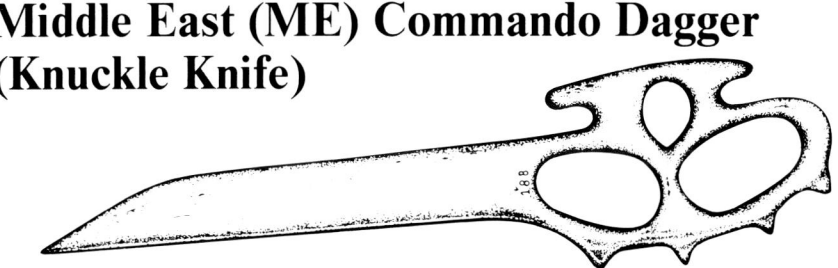

To further confuse Axis intelligence about the purpose of Layforce — the seizure of Rhodes — the units were referred to as "battalions" as follows:

- A Battalion - #7 Commando
- B Battalion - #8 Commando
- C Battalion - #11 Commando
- D Battalion - #50 and #52 ME Commandos

In preparation for the Rhodes operation Roger Courtney's Folbot Section (the forerunner of the SBS) carried out a reconnaissance of the island. The invasion of Greece by the Germans on 6 April, however, forced the cancellation of the Rhodes operation, and Layforce was given the new mission of striking behind German lines in North Africa in an attempt to stall Rommel.

On the night of 19/20 April, A 'Battalion' carried out a raid on Bardia. But, due to problems in landing and poor intelligence, the operation was not entirely successful, however, the Commandos managed to blow up a bridge and burn an Italian tire dump. Unfortunately, sixty-seven Commandos did not reach the correct beach for extraction and were taken prisoner. Still, the operation caused a German armored brigade to be diverted and tied down defending Bardia, removing them from Rommel's striking force.

In May, A and D Battalions were taken out of the Commando role and placed in the General Reserve while C Battalion was sent to Cyprus. This left only B Battalion in the raiding role. When the Germans invaded Crete on 20 May 1941, it was decided to use part of Layforce to aid in the counterattack. In effect, however, Layforce acted as a covering force for the British withdrawal. While acting as the rear guard for the retreat, Layforce saw very heavy action acquitting themselves well. However, because they had to hold their defensive positions to cover the evacuation on the beaches, most of the Layforce Commandos on Crete were taken prisoner. Less than 200 were evacuated.

In June of 1941 C Battalion of Layforce was involved in the invasion of Vichy French controlled Syria. The Commandos' mission was to seize and hold crossings over the Litani River. C Battalion met heavy resistance, suffering twenty-five percent casualties, but managed to advance to the key crossing point, only to have the French blow the bridge just as the main body approached. A detachment of B Battalion took part in the defense of Tobruk when it came under siege by the Germans in April of 1941.

In August of 1941 Layforce was disbanded. Some of its members later formed Mission 204 which worked with the Chinese in Burma, while others joined David Sterling to form the nucleus of the Special Air Service (SAS). Churchill still wanted a Commando capability in the Middle East, however, so it wasn't long before a new Middle East Commando was formed under Laycock. The new unit consisted of:

Hq and Depot - based at Geneifa
#2 Troop - L Detachment, SAS
#3 Troop - remnants of Layforce
#4 Troop - Palestinians formerly in #51 ME Commando
#5 Troop - Palestinians formerly in #51 ME Commando
#6 Troop - the SBS

During OPERATION CRUSADER to relieve Tobruk, #3 Troop was assigned to raid Rommel's headquarters on the night of 17/18 November. Their intelligence was faulty, however, and they hit the wrong house, missing Rommel. Still, they managed to kill some staff officers in the raid and left the Germans uneasy by a raid so far in their rear. After this raid many of the Commandos were captured, but some were able to infiltrate back through the desert. It took Laycock himself forty-one days to get back.

By August of 1942 the Middle East Commandos had pretty well ceased to exist with special forces activities in the Middle East being handled by the SAS, SBS, Long Range Desert Group (LRDG), Popski's Private Army, and other such units.

Operations in the Mediterranean 1943-1945

During the last two months of 1942, #1 and #6 Commandos carried out amphibious operations during the Allied advance into Tunisia following OPERATION TORCH. Later, however, these two commandos were given critical defensive assignments. #6 Commando helped to hold out against German paratroopers advancing after the Battle of the Kasserine Pass. Because of the attrition suffered by these two commando units, at least partially due to the lack of heavy support weapons, #1 and #6 Commandos were pulled back to Great Britain in April of 1943.

Another commando unit involved in the Tunisian campaign was #30 Commando, a specialized intelligence gathering unit. Later, this specialized commando received both small boat and parachute training to increase its versatility. #33 Troop of #30 Commando often operated alongside lead troops during advances so they could take charge of important documents, prisoners, etc., as soon as they were taken. In some cases, #33 Troop, demonstrating the commando spirit, attacked and took key objectives themselves. During 7 to 9 May 1943 #33 Troop took 250 prisoners.

Commandos were also involved in OPERATION HUSKY, the landings on Sicily. In preparation for these landings, #3 Commando, which had been in Gibraltar was sent to Algiers. Other commandos slated for involvement in the landings were #2, #40 (RM), and #41 (RM) Commandos, with all four coming under the command of Laycock. Commandos taking part in HUSKY were organized into five troops, each with three officers and sixty-two other ranks, and a heavy weapons troop, which was armed with two 3-inch mortars and two Vickers machine guns. On Sicily #3 Commando was slated to land ahead of 5th Division, #40 and #41 Commandos were scheduled to go in ahead of the Canadians, while #2 Commando was to act as a floating reserve.

The landings took place on 10 July. #40 and #41 Commandos went in on the left flank of the Canadians at about 0300, and by 0500 had achieved their objectives. By 0800 they had taken up defensive positions to hold the flank. By 0600 #3 Commando had captured the key battery they had been assigned to take out. Later, on 13 July, #3 Commando was re-embarked and landed to seize a key bridge over the Lentini River. Although #3 Commando suffered 153 casualties, they accomplished their mission and kept the Germans from blowing the critical bridge.

As the Allies continued on the offensive in the Mediterranean Commandos found more and more employment for their amphibious skills. #2 and #41 (RM) Commandos took part in OPERATION AVALANCHE, the landings at Salerno. Commandos were landed in advance of AVALANCHE to gather intelligence along the coast, while others were assigned key objectives during the initial assault. The Special Service Brigade HQ, #2, and #41 (RM) Commandos sailed from Palermo, Sicily on 8 September and landed in the early hours of 9 September. #2 captured their objective, an artillery battery that was undefended. As #2 and #41 (RM) Commandos advanced, however, they met heavy opposition and had to fight off enemy counterattacks. At times the lightly armed Commandos were forced to engage German tanks with grenades, and #41 (RM) Commando holding Vietri came under especially heavy attack. Within a couple of days, conventional infantry had taken over from the Commandos, allowing them to go into reserve, but they were thrown back into combat almost immediately. Finally, on 18/19 September, #2 and #41 were relieved and sent back to Sicily. While committed at Salerno they had suffered fifty percent casualties.

During September of 1943 #3 and #40 (RM) Commandos took part in OPERATION BAYTOWN, the landings across the Strait of Messina.

#3 and #40 (RM) Commandos were in action again on 2/3 October as part of OPERATION DEVON, being given the mission of capturing the port of Termoli with an assault from the sea, obviously an operation worthy of their mettle. #3's mission was to capture a beachhead west of Termoli and hold it, while #40 was to pass through the beachhead and capture the town. By 0800 on 3 October the town had been captured, which Commandos held until being reinforced, and remained to help fight off counterattacks, during which the Commandos took a number of casualties.

In November of 1943 #3 and #41 (RM) Commandos returned to England to rebuild after the heavy casualties suffered at Salerno and Termoli. To replace them #9 and #43 (RM) Commandos were sent out from the UK. #2 Commando remained in the Mediterranean and was brought up to strength with local recruits who received their commando training at Molfetta. During this reorganization, Brigadier Tom Churchill, who had been temporarily commanding 2 Special Service Brigade was given permanent command. Also in December, #4 (Belgian) and #6 (Polish) Troops of #10 Commando were sent out to join #2 Special Service Brigade.

Early in 1943, #30 Commando had received additional training in intelligence gathering, and during OPERATION HUSKY #30 was assigned key radar stations as their targets, where they captured some very important documents. #30 Commando also

(Above) Members of #40 (RM) Commando unloading on Malta are wearing Royal Marine beret badges, camouflage smocks, and are armed with Lee Enfield rifles.

A pair Royal Marine Commandos during the advance between Salerno and Naples have time for a break to read a newspaper and write a letter amidst their duffle bags.

(Below) Commandos of either #40 (RM) or #41 (RM) Commando in Italy between Salerno and Naples. Unlike Army Commandos, which by this time were heavily armed with Thompson SMGs, most of the Royal Marine Commandos were still armed with Lee Enfield rifles.

Royal Marine Commando Cap Badge

Royal Marine Commando Shoulder Patch

took part in the Salerno landings where they seized documents relating to torpedo research and carried out reconnaissance missions.

Late in 1943, #9 Commando was used for operations in Italy, including reconnaissance of islands off the coast of Italy and raids along the Rapido River. Belgian and Polish Commando Troops, formerly of #10 (Inter Allied Commando), began operations in the Mediterranean late in 1943 as well.

In January of 1944, #2 Special Service Brigade less #2 Commando, set up a base near Castellamare in Western Italy. From this base various commandos carried out operations in Italy and elsewhere in the Mediterranean. On 17 January #40 (RM) Commando aided the 56th Division in crossing the River Garigliano. On the night of 21/22 January #9 Commando and #43 (RM) Commando landed first at Anzio to seize the critical high ground. The Commandos linked up with their American counterparts — the Rangers — the next day, and were withdrawn back to Naples by 25 January. Shortly after #9 and #43 (RM) Commandos were pulled from Anzio elements of #2 SS Brigade were used to seize Monte Ornito. After the Monte Ornito operation #40 (RM) Commando joined #2 SS Brigade and #43 (RM) Commando was detached and sent for operations in the Adriatic.

By 2 March, #9 and #40 (RM) Commandos were committed at Anzio under the 56th Division, with #40 being used primarily for offensive patrolling and #9 being used for a local attack before they were both withdrawn on 25 March.

While #2 SS Brigade was setting up shop at Castellamare, #2 Commando was aiding Yugoslav partisans by operating from the island of Vis as a primary component of Force 133. By 12 February 1944 all of #2 Commando, along with members of #7 (Yugoslav) Troop of #10 Commando and some OSS agents were on Vis. Later they were joined on Vis by other units including a light AA battery and a machine gun detachment from the Raiding Support Regiment. At the end of February, #43 (RM) Commando arrived at Vis to give Force 133 even more striking power. Raids had already begun in late January of 1944, even before all of #2 Commando had arrived, with the German-held islands off of the Yugoslav coast being targets of both raiding and reconnaissance missions by the commandos. Early in March, in anticipation of a German invasion of the island, the HQ of #2 SS Brigade and the remainder of the Raiding Support Regiment were deployed to Vis.

A very successful raid on the night of 17/18 March by #2 Commando and elements of #43 (RM) Commando, however, helped to force the Germans onto the defensive, preventing them from invading Vis. This raid was followed a few days later by highly successful raid against Hvar by part of #43 (RM) Commando and a group of partisans. During this raid fifty of the enemy were killed and eighty captured for only twenty-one Partisan and Commando casualties.

As preparations proceeded for the invasion of France, the Belgian Commando Troop which had been operating in Italy returned to the UK and the Polish Troop joined II Polish Corps in Italy. While serving with II Corps, the Polish Commandos were known as the 2nd Motorized Commando Battalion. The Polish Commandos fought very well throughout the campaign in Italy, especially at Monte Cassino.

#40 (RM) Commando arrived on Vis in May of 1944 to reinforce the raiding units already on the island. Also in May, seventy-five men of #9 Commando carried out a classical special forces mission when they rescued 120 allied POWs. When the Partisans on the mainland found themselves under heavy pressure from a German offensive in early June of 1944, #40 (RM) Commando, #43 (RM) Command, and elements of the Raiding Support Regiment carried out operations against the German garrison at Barc. The Commandos suffered heavy casualties, but managed to relieve the pressure on the Partisans.

In July, #2 Commando and #40 (RM) Commando were pulled back from Vis. With #2 Commando immediately preparing for operations in Albania. In August #40 Commando was sent to Malta.

Royal Marine Commandos during the advance up the length of Italy compare souvenirs. The shoulder arcs that can be seen on the Commandos at the right and left are different, and neither wears the Combined Operations roundel.

During August of 1944, #43 (RM) Commando continued to operate from Vis, and as the Germans began leaving the island of Barc the Commandos landed on Barc to harass the German withdrawal.

In late July, #2 Comando was sent into Albania. With #2 and the Raiding Support Regiment being needed to help destroy the German garrison at Spilje so arms could be gotten in to the Partisans via the coast. Although the Commandos met heavy resistance they did help open up the coast of Albania to the Partisans.

#9 Commando, meanwhile, destroyed a bridge linking the islands of Lussino Piccolo and Lussino Grande in August of 1944. In September #9 landed on the island of Kithera.

On the night of 21/22 September #2 Commando, along with #40 (RM) Commando, landed in Albania to support the Partisans in attacking the German garrison at Sarande. This operation was successful, and the Commandos were ordered to follow the Germans during their retreat northward through Albania. When the Germans had been driven from Albania, the Commandos were ordered back to Italy with #40 (RM) Commando remaining on Corfu.

General Montgomery presents a Member of #46 (RM) Commando with the Military Medal. The Commando wears a Combined Operations roundel and both the Royal Marines and the Commando shoulder arcs.

Belgian Commandos of #10 (IA) Commando in Italy wear Belgian lion beret badges. The Commando to the right of center has a rather efficient method of slinging his Thompson SMG.

Belgians of #10 (IA) Commando in Italy stop for chow; note the insignia worn on the forearm of the trooper in the foreground.

As the Germans pulled out of Greece and the Greek islands, #9 Commando was ordered to the Greek mainland to help prevent a civil war, while #40 performed the same mission on Corfu. By February of 1945, however, #9 Commando was free to return to Italy.

In October of 1944, #43 (RM) Commando had been sent to harry the retreating Germans in the mountains of Montenegro, Yugoslavia. In January of 1945, however, #43 was withdrawn when the Yugoslavians pressed to handle their own liberation.

With the Germans driven from most of the Mediterranean by early 1945, the bulk of #2 Commando Brigade's raiding targets had disappeared. As a result, #2, #9, #40 (RM), and #43 (RM) Commandos operated as infantry in Italy during February and March of 1945.

In April of 1945, however, all four Commandos took part in an operation more suitable to their skills when they were used to help force a crossing of Lake Commachio. And once the crossing had been made the Commandos helped open a gap through which the armored forces could pour. This was the final action for #2 Commando Brigade, which had spent almost two years operating in the Mediterranean and had suffered almost 1,500 casualties.

A Belgian Commando of #10 (IA) Commando in Italy holds a Lee Enfield #4 Mark 1(T) sniper's rifle and carries a 36M (Mills Bomb) grenade on his belt. Many of these Belgian Commandos wear the leather jerkin and carry their toggle ropes across the back of their necks.

Belgians of #10 (IA) Commando in Italy move out. The sergeant at right wears an F-S dagger on his left thigh, and each of the Commandos wears a beret and carries a steel helmet for combat.

(Above) Commandos come ashore at Anzio with their bicycles which provided a great deal of speed and mobility. Due to heavy shelling in the Anzio beachhead steel helmets were wisely chosen over Green berets.

(Right) Commandos at Anzio clean a Thompson SMG and load spare magazines with .45 caliber ammunition.

(Below) Members of #9 Commando at Anzio beach load new Bren gun magazines with .303 ammunition in anticipation of action during early 1944.

(Above) Bren gunner of #9 Commando at Anzio carries the light machinegun, which was so popular with the Commandos, on a shoulder sling.

(Above) A Commando Bren gunner at Anzio carries a Colt .45 automatic tucked into his belt for easy access, a smart move since the issue holster was very slow and the lanyard attached to the gun's butt prevented its loss.

(Right) This trooper of #9 Commando at Anzio wears the tough leather jerkin and carries a Thompson on a sling.

(Above) #9 Commandos during a perimeter patrol at Anzio early in 1944, better trained and disciplined, the Commandos were ideal for, and carried out aggressive patrols.

(Above Right) After a night patrol men of #9 Commando are picked up at their rendezvous point by a jeep. Anzio 1944.

No. 2 Commando Beret Badges

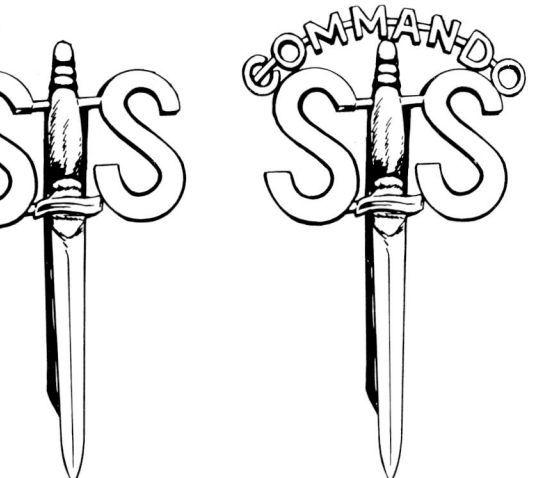

Troopers of #9 Commando enjoy a hot cup of tea after returning from a night patrol.

This Commando working with Partisans in Albania carries the rugged hard hitting Colt .45 automatic, a favorite hand gun among Commandos.

Commandos firing at the enemy in Albania. The Commando on the right is using an Enfield sniper rifle.

An Albanian farmer supplies a drink of water to a Commando armed with a Sten SMG. The helmet netting allowed local foliage to be carried on the helmet as camouflage.

Commandos, believed to be of #30 Commando, talk with a rather affable Albanian soldier. The Commando second from the right wears a rather odd beret badge, and SAS wings are worn on the right sleeve of the man at the left.

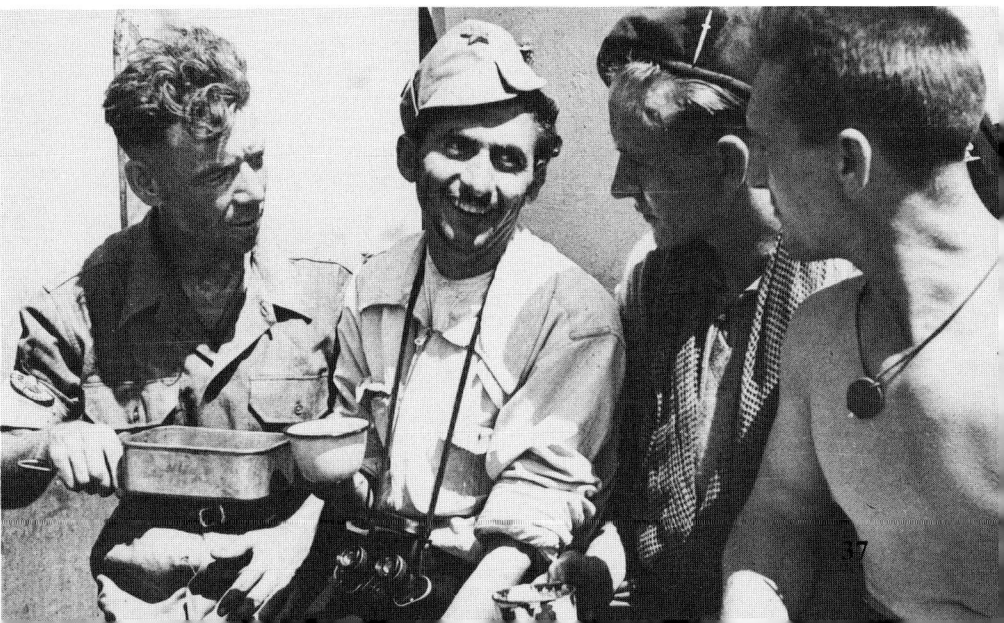

Members of #9 Commando, most of which are armed with Lee-Enfield rifles, are embarking for a raid on Cherso Island in August of 1944.

#9 Commandos sort out their equipment on the deck of the Motor Torpedo Boat (MTB) before it pulls out for Cherso Island. The Commando at left not only wears rubber boots but also a life jacket.

The MTB is overall Light Grey with heavy splashes of Dark Gray to break up its silhouette. The torpedo tubes are covered with tarps.

Commandos taking part in the Cherso Island raid stow their folding bicycles onto the MTB; Commandos often used these folding bicycles to cover ground quickly.

Preparations for Overlord
Through The Conquest of Germany

During the spring of 1943 the Small Scale Raiding Force was disbanded, with most of its members being absorbed into either Combined Operations Assault Pilotage Parties (COPPs) or #12 Commando. Early in 1943 Commando operations into Norway had resumed, with most operations being carried out by members of North Force who were drawn from various units and had attended the Commando Mountain and Snow Warfare Training Center at Braemar, Scotland. By February of 1943 North Force consisted of B and D Troops of #12 Commando, the Norwegian Troop of #10 (IA) Commando, a Boat Troop of #14 Commando, and a small contingent from #30 Commando. Operations into Norway were usually launched from the Shetland Islands. On 23/24 January 1943, for example, D Troop of #12 Commando along with Norwegian Commandos attacked the pyrite mines on the island of Stord. Over the next few weeks North Force mounted additional raids against Norway, and while most of the objectives had some importance to the German war effort, the primary aim was to tie down as many German troops as possible in Norway so they could not be used to reinforce the defenses of France.

As Commando landings increased in size the role of the Commandos changed. In April of 1943, Laycock suggested a reorganization scheme. Among other suggestions was the formation of a Holding Commando for men who had completed Commando training in which they could serve until they were needed as replacements by an operational unit. The Commandos would go through two reorganizations during 1943 resulting in the following order of battle by the end of the year.

Special Service Group HQ (along with the training and holding establishments and certain specialized troops directly attached to HQ) were under Group Commander — Major General R.G. Sturges, Royal Marines

1st Special Service Brigade (based in Sussex) - #3, #4, #6, and #44 (RM) Commandos.

2nd Special Service Brigade (based in Italy) - #2, #9, #40, (RM), and #43 (RM) Commandos

3rd Special Service Brigade (based in India) - #1, #5, #42 (RM), and #44 (RM) Commandos

4th Special Service Brigade (based in Kent) - #10 (Inter Allied), #41 (RM), #46 (RM) and #47 (RM) Commandos

During the spring and summer of 1943 a number of raids under the cover name FORFAR were launched against the French coast to gather intelligence and to capture prisoners in preparation for the planned invasion of France during 1944. Many of the Commandos assigned to these operations had received parachute training, and at least one of the groups was inserted via parachute. During the fall of 1943 'Timberforce' was formed to carry out further raids in Norway to insure that German garrisons remained there or were even strengthened.

Late December saw operations again increased along the French coast. These raids were divided into two distinct types of missions — 'Hardtack', which were reconnaissance, and 'Manacle', which were basically prisoner snatches. Hardtack and Manacle operations were carried out by 'Layforce II' under the command of Robert Laycock's brother Major Peter Laycock. To keep the Germans off balance two or three such operations per night were mounted. Early in 1944, however, 'Hardtack' and 'Manacle' raids were cancelled in the fear that they would lead the Germans to strengthen the French coastal defenses in response.

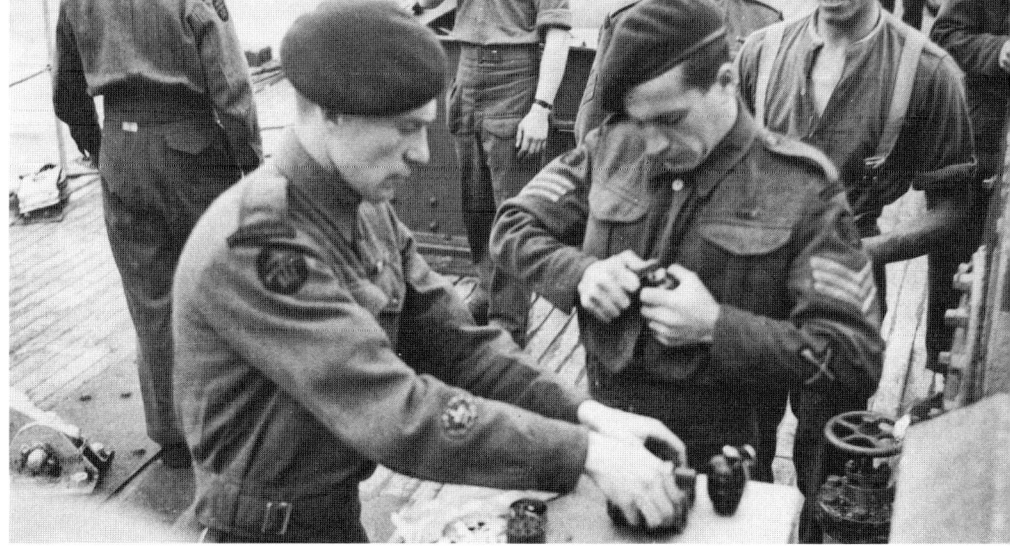

Commandos prepare grenades aboard ship prior to their landing on the beaches of Normandy; the sergeant at right wears the crossed rifles of a weapons instructor on his sleeve.

As plans for OVERLORD, the Allied invasion of Europe, were formulated in early 1944 it was decided that eight Commandos would be needed to support the landings by Montgomery's 21st Army Group. However, since only seven Commandos were readily available, #48 (RM) Commando was hurriedly raised and trained for the landings. By the end of March, the 1st Special Service Brigade (#3, #4, #6, and #45 (RM) Commandos) under the command of Brigadier Lord Lovat and the 4th Special Service Brigade (#41 (RM), #46 (RM), #47 (RM), and #48 (RM) Commandos) under Brigadier B.W. Leicester were assigned to the 21st Army Group in preparation for the Normandy landings.

The 1st Special Service Brigade, two French Troops of #10 (IA) Commando, and #41 (RM) Commando were assigned to spearhead the landings at 'Sword' Beach; #46 (RM) Commando and #48 (RM) Commando were assigned to 'Juno' Beach, and #47 (RM) Commando was assigned to 'Gold' Beach. While most raids against the French Coast had been curtailed during the months preceding D-Day, 'Tarbrush' raids by #3 Troop of #10 (IA) Commando were carried out in May of 1944, along the Pas de Calais coast to gain information on the types of mines being used by the Germans and to give the impression that the invasion would come along this portion of the coast.

On D-Day the 1st Special Service Brigade was assigned the mission of landing in the Ouistreham area of Sword, pushing inland to link up with the 6th Airborne Division, then cover the left flank of Sword Beach. #41 (RM) and #48 (RM) Commandos were to destroy coastal defenses near Lion-sur-Mer and St. Aubin between Juno and Sword, and then seize the radar station at Douvres with members of #30 Commando searching the radar station for intelligence information. #47 (RM) Commando was to capture Port-en-Bessin on the right flank of Gold Beach. #46 (RM) Commando was held in reserve for possible use in cliff assaults against the coastal batteries near Orne.

In preparation for D-Day the various commandos went through specialist refresher training courses. The 1st Special Service Brigade and #47 (RM) Commando worked on speed marching; #41 (RM) and #48 (RM) Commandos honed their building clearing and street fighting skills; and #46 (RM) Commando polished their cliff scaling skills. #3 (Misc.) Troop of #10 (IA) Commando was to be used for infiltration missions due to the large number of German speaking members.

Commandos taking part in OPERATION OVERLORD embarked on LCI(S)s on 5 June. The first troops ashore on the morning of 6 June 1944 was #4 Commando at 0820 hours. #6 Commando along with Lord Lovat and his HQ landed at 0840 and pushed inland to link up with the paratroopers holding a bridge on the road to Breville and then moved on to Breville itself, with Lord Lovat's piper leading the advance. #3 and #45 (RM) Commandos landed at 0910. Once ashore, #3 Commando advanced toward the village of Le Plein to help the paratroopers take the Village. #3 Troop on bicycles advanced rapidly, providing support to the paratroopers. #45 (RM) Commando pushed to Merville where they dug in after relieving the paratroopers holding the village. By the end of the day on 6 June, the 1st Special Service Brigade had not reached all of its objectives but they had linked up with the airborne troops and helped secure the bridges across the Orne River.

While the Commandos of the 1st Special Service Brigade were landing and driving to the Orne River, the 4th Special Service Brigade HQ and #48 (RM) Commando landed at St. Aubin and advanced to Langrune on the first day. #41 (RM) Commando landed and pushed to Luc-sur-Mer before the end of the first day. While #47 (RM) Commando lost almost twenty percent of its strength when four LCAs were sunk off the beaches, the remainder of the commando fought on toward the objective of Port-en-Bessin but did not manage to take it until the next day.

On 7 June, D-Day plus one, the commandos of the 1st Special Service Brigade tried to consolidate their positions. #45 (RM) Commando was pulled back from Merville to more defensible lines, but then was sent to take Franceville-Plage, but had to be withdrawn to Merville.

#4 Special Service Brigade continued to push forward on the 7th, with #41 (RM) Commando taking Luc-sur-Mer, #47 (RM) Commando taking Port-en-Bessin, and #48 (RM) Commando taking Langrune. #46 (RM) Commando had been in reserve, but on D-Day plus one #46 (RM) landed and drove inland to link up with #41 (RM) Commando and then advanced toward the radar station at Douvres.

#1 Special Service Brigade was still encountering heavy opposition on 8 June, but by 10 June German resistance began to slacken. #4 Commando had particularly borne the brunt of heavy German counterattacks.

During July and August as heavier allied units broke out of the Normandy beachhead, the Commandos continued to guard the left flank of the beachhead. During this period aggressive patrolling by the Commandos discouraged German counterattacks against their positions. As OPERATION GOODWIND — a breakout thrust by three armored divisions - was launched on 18 July, the Commandos and Sixth Airborne Division protecting the flank became even more important as the Allied supply lines began to stretch forward.

Beginning on 19 August, both Special Service Brigades took part in the eastward advance toward the Seine River. The 1st Special Service Brigade halted at Beuzeville and on 7 September returned to Britain. The 4th Special Service Brigade crossed the Seine River on 31 August and then helped contain the German garrison at Dunkirk.

#30 Commando — the intelligence gathering Commando — had been operating primarily with the Americans. A and B Troops plus the HQ were with Patton during his breakout, and by September the HQ, and A and X Troops were in Paris. B Troop meanwhile, was involved in the capture of Brest. Part of A Troop managed to take part in the capture of Le Havre. Throughout the advance across France, #30 Commando had gathered intelligence wherever possible and by the end of September had pulled out of the battle and returned to Britain with all of its captured material.

Upon its return to the UK in September of 1944, members of 1st Special Service Brigade received a long-awaited leave, while new recruits were sought for both of the Special Service Brigades. Between 6 June and 30 September 1944 the two Commando

Commandos link up with glider-borne troops on D-Day, 6 June 1944 and have brought several somewhat unwilling guests. From the cap badges, these Commandos appear to be from one of the Royal Marine Commandos. A light motorcycle is strapped to the hood of the jeep.

brigades had sustained more than fifty percent casualties, and while many of the wounded would return to action, the strength of many of the Commandos was sorely depleted. So depleted was #46 (RM) Commando that at the end of September it had to be pulled back to Britain and replaced by #4 Commando of #4 Special Service Brigade.

The Dutch Troop of #10 Commando made one of the few Commando parachute jumps of the war when they jumped at Arnhem during OPERATION MARKET GARDEN as part of the plan to liberate Belgium and Holland. However, before the Low Countries could be liberated it was necessary to open the Port of Antwerp, which meant taking the fortress on the island of Walcheren. The plan for capturing the fort called for

Near the Orne River on 17 June 1944 Brigadier Peter Young briefs two Commando snipers. The sniper at left wears a mesh tunic and hood, to which foliage can be easily attached. This camouflaged mesh with foliage attached could to help a sniper to virtually disappear.

This hard looking French Naval Infantry Commando assigned to #4 Commando took part in the liberation of France. It is doubtful that a German POW would consider himself fortunate to fall into his hands if indeed this Frenchman deigned to take prisoners.

#41 (RM), #47 (RM), and #48 (RM) Commandos along with #4 (Belgian) Troop and #5 (Norwegian) Troop of #10 (IA) Commando to land on the west side of the island at West Kapelle, while #4 Commando and two French troops of #10 (IA) Commando would attack from the south at Flushing. On 1 November 1944 the operation was launched. Once ashore the Commandos had to fight from strongpoint to strongpoint. By the time the operation was completed and the Germans surrendered, the Commandos had suffered almost 500 casualties, but by the end of November the port of Antwerp was in use by the Allies. #46 (RM) Commando was temporarily sent to Antwerp to guard against the possibility of a German paratrooper assault, but returned in time for the crossing of the Rhine in March of 1945.

In December of 1944 the Special Service Group was redesignated the Commando Group and the Special Service Brigades became Commando Brigades. During December of 1944 when the Germans launched their Ardennes Offensive, #47 (RM) and #48 (RM) Commandos were sent to reinforce defenses along the Maas River.

In January of 1945 #1 Commando Brigade was ordered back to the continent in order to provide amphibious assault capability for crossing river barriers during the final drive into Germany.

Commandos were committed to OPERATION PLUNDER, the Rhine crossing at Wessel. The 1st Commando Brigade secured the Allied right flank, and on 23 March #46 (RM) Commando led the assault and secured a temporary bridgehead downstream from Wessel. Other Commandos then crossed to support #46 and additional reinforcements arrived when U.S. paratroopers of the 17th Airborne Division jumped east of Wessel. As the allies thrust deeper into Germany, #1 Commando Brigade was placed under 6th Airborne Division, but by 6 April the Brigade was serving under the 11th Armored Division ready to spearhead the crossing of the Weser River. After successfully crossing the Weser the commandos went on to seize a bridge across the River Aller on the night of 10/11 April.

On 28 April 1945 the 1st Commando Brigade continued to lead the advance as they spearheaded the crossing of the Elbe river for the 15th Scottish Division. First across the river was #6 Commando, followed by #46 (RM) Commando. This was the final major operation of the Commandos in Europe. During the final months of the war #4 Commando Brigade had primarily been used to carry out patrols and reconnaissance missions. #30 Assault Unit (as #30 Commando came to be known) had returned to the Continent for the thrust into Germany and charged with gathering intelligence about submarines, torpedoes, and technical exchanges with Japan as its top priority. #30 Assault Unit was among the first allied troops into Cologne, Kiel, Wilhelmshaven, Bremen, and other important cities. A coup of #30 Assault Unit was the capture of sixteen advanced German submarines under construction at Deschimag Shipyard in Bremen.

Carrying a Thompson SMG, this French Commando takes time to be welcomed by his countrymen.

Royal Marine Commandos during the hard fought Walchern Island battle that opened up the port of Antwerp in November of 1944. American supplied Amtracks are in the background.

Men of #2 Commando Brigade release message carrying pigeons. While this form of communications is thousands of years old it still proves to be extremely useful.

Field Marshal Alexander reviewing members of #9 Commando. Wearing parade uniforms the Commandos wear a cockade on their berets rather than a beret badge.

Commandos taking part in the Rhine crossing at Wesel in March of 1945 study a map, possibly to see how much further it is to Berlin.

Commando machine gunners lay down suppressing fire during the Rhine crossings from a water cooled machine gun. Three men were an absolute necessity on this heavy weapon, not only to carry it (one to carry the ammunition, one to carry the tripod, and one to carry the machine gun), but also to fire it (an observer to sight it with binoculars, one to feed the ammunition, and a third to fire the machinegun).

Fairbairn-Sykes Dagger (3rd Pattern)

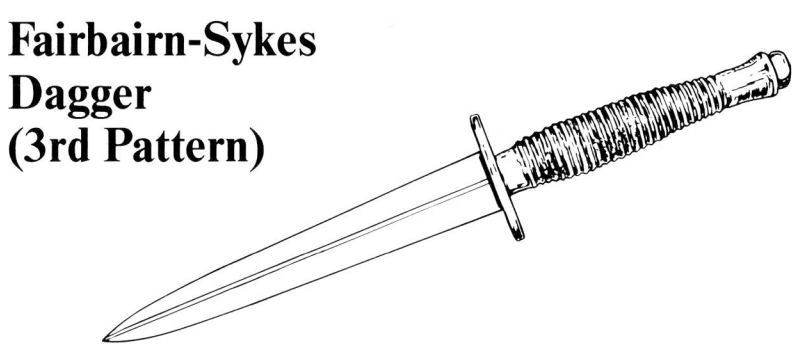

Commandos taking a break during the Lake Commachio operation in April of 1945, check the co-ordinates on their map, and check in with headquarters on the radio.

(Above) Commandos of the Royal Marine Commandos, wearing what appear to be Denison camouflage smocks, land during the Lake Commachio crossings.

(Above Right) These Commandos during the Lake Commachio crossing in April of 1945 seem to have forgotten the axiom about 'bunching up' and getting killed.

Webley Mk 6 .455 Caliber Revolver

Colt M1911 A1 .45 Caliber Pistol

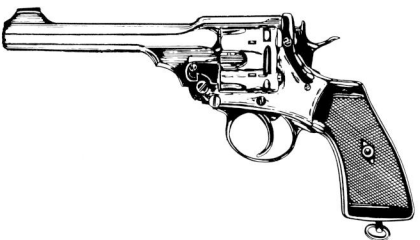
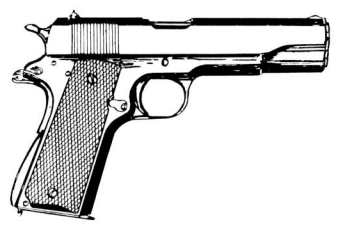

(Left) Commandos fanning out along the shore of Lake Commachio. The two lead troopers are carrying Thompson SMGs.

(Right) Commandos advance into the country side after crossing Lake Commachio. A radio, with its arial extended, is carried by the Commando at the right.

The Far East

In August of 1943 Lord Mountbatten set up the Southeast Asia Command, and since Mountbatten had seen first hand the value of Commandos during his time with Combined Operations in Europe, he quickly requested a Special Service Brigade be assigned to his command. In December of 1943 Brigadier W.I. Nonweiler, commanding the 3rd Special Service Brigade, went to India to prepare for the deployment of his brigade. First to arrive were #5 and #44 (RM) Commandos on 19 December 1943. In mid-January #1 and #42 (RM) Commandos, which had been delayed because of damage suffered to their transport in the Mediterranean, joined the brigade. Also joining the brigade was #2 (Dutch) Troop of #10 (IA) Commando, which was intended for operations in the Dutch East Indies. The 3rd Special Service Brigade was based at Kedgaon near Poona.

#5 and #44 (RM) Commandos were used in OPERATION SCREWDRIVER during March of 1944, landing in the Japanese rear to help with the drive to clear the Maungdaw-Buthidaung Road along the coast of Burma. The operation was successful, but the Commandos found the Japanese to be exceedingly tough opponents. A few weeks later, on 11 April 1944, #5 and #44 (RM) Commandos were rushed to Silchar to help counter a Japanese offensive. For the next four months these two Commandos mounted aggressive patrols into the Assam hills to prevent a Japanese build up prior to another offensive. While #5 and #44 (RM) Commandos had been in action against the Japanese, #1 and #42 (RM) Commandos had been undergoing rigorous jungle training.

In September all four Commandos of the 3rd Special Service Brigade were sent to Ceylon, although #2 (Dutch) Troop returned to the UK to be available for the liberation of Holland. The 3rd SS Brigade only remained in Ceylon a few weeks before returning for more operations in the Arakan. By December of 1944 IV Indian Corps was about to go on the offensive, and it was decided to use #3 Commando Brigade in amphibious assaults to outflank the Japanese.

The first major amphibious operation was mounted on the Myebon Peninsula on 12 January 1945. First ashore was #42 (RM) Commando which encountered heavy mud and anti-personnel mines, but managed to secure the beachhead quickly. #5 and and then #1 Commandos passed through, moving inland against fanatical Japanese resistance. Finally, on 13 January #44 (RM) Commando came ashore to reinforce the beachhead. By 18 June #3 Commando Brigade had secured most of the peninsula and had mopped up local resistance.

Once the Myebon Peninsula was secure, the Japanese were left with only the Myobaung-Tamandu Road as a retreat route from the Arakan. #3 Commando Brigade was ordered to cut the road at Kangaw, and landings began at 1300 on 22 January 1945. #1 Commando was first ashore this time, seizing a critical hill overlooking the bridgehead. #42 (RM) Commando followed, seizing the actual bridgehead, with #5 Commando moving through to support #1 Commando. #44, in reserve, was later used to capture an objective near the beachhead. During the night of 22/23 January, the Japanese launched a vicious counterattack against #1 Commando, which was finally halted in hand-to-hand combat, at which the Commandos excelled. Conventional infantry began coming ashore to reinforce the beachhead. #44 (RM) Commando suffered heavy casualties on the night of 23/24 January when they were hit by heavy counterattacks. As late as 31 January, #42 (RM) had to fight off another Japanese counterattack, but by early February the Commandos had completed their mission and were withdrawn from Kangaw.

There were plans to use #3 Commando Brigade in OPERATION ZIPPER (the invasion of Malaya), but the war ended first. Instead, #3 Commando brigade was sent to Hong Kong in September to help accept the Japanese surrender.

Sten Gun Mk 2 With Silencer

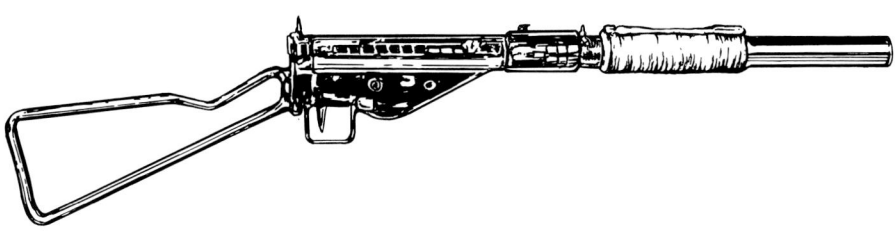

Royal Marine Commandos

The Royal Marines have traditionally been Britain's amphibious forces, and this role was continued during World War II. The Royal Marine (Amphibious) Brigade was formed in December of 1939, with the Royal Marines taking part in the campaign in Narvik, while other Royal Marines were sent to Dakar during the summer of 1940. The early days of the war against Japan saw many Royal Marines become part of ad hoc 'commando' units used to delay the Japanese advance.

In December of 1941 the Special Service Platoon, formed from the Royal Marine detachment off the Prince of Wales (sunk on 10 December 1941), was used on raiding missions and helped in the defense of Singapore. Early in 1942, another ad hoc unit, 'Force Viper', operated in Burma. Large contingents of Royal Marines were also involved in the invasion of Madagascar. The original Royal Marine Commando was raised at Deal on 14 February 1942. This Commando took heavy casualties in the Dieppe landings and was rebuilt as #40 (RM) Commando. Other Royal Marine Commandos were formed from Royal Marine battalions on the following dates:

#41 (RM) Commando - October, 1942
#42 (RM) Commando - August, 1943
#43 (RM) Commando - August, 1943
#44 (RM) Commando - August, 1943
#45 (RM) Commando - August, 1943
#46 (RM) Commando - August, 1943
#47 (RM) Commando - August, 1943
#48 (RM) Commando - March, 1944

Normal strength of a Royal Marine Commando was about 450 men. By 1944 a Royal Marine Commando Troop consisted of sixty Commandos broken into an HQ and two Sections. The section normally consisted of two eleven man Assault Sub-Sections and a five-man Support Sub-Section, with the latter containing the Section mortar and a sniper. Bren gunners were included in each Assault Sub-Section. This organization provided each Troop with a lot of firepower and great flexibility.

During the post-war years the Royal Marine Commandos have carried on the Commando tradition in #3 Commando Brigade, which, unlike the wartime Commando Brigades, consists of only three Commandos. After the war it was decided to retain one Commando from each of the major theaters of World War II so that the traditions and battle honors would be retained — #3 Commando Brigade is comprised of #40 (RM) Commando representing the Mediterranean/Middle East, #42 (RM) Commando representing the Far East, and #45 (RM) Commando representing Northwest Europe.

Two other units of note are the Royal Marine Boom Patrol Detachment and the Royal Marine Detachment 385. The Boom Patrol Detachment used canoes and were trained to infiltrate enemy harbors to sink shipping using limpet mines. By far, the most famous raid carried out by the Boom Patrol Detachment was the 'Cockleshell Heroes' raid of Bordeaux Harbor in December of 1942, sinking German blockade runners carrying advanced German technology to Japan. Six two-man Cockle Mk II canoes were supposed to be launched on the night of 7/8 December 1942 from the submarine **Tuna**, but one Cockle had its rubberized canvas skin slit so only five canoes were launched. The raiders had to paddle more than seventy miles up the Gironde to place their charges. Four German ships were severely damaged in the raid, but only one of the crews managed to escape with the help of the French Resistance. The other four crews were either drowned, or captured and shot per Hitler's 'Commando Order'.

The Boom Patrol Detachment was later used for raids in the Mediterranean. Other members of the unit received radio and parachute training, and were dropped onto islands in the Aegean or Adriatic.

Royal Marine Detachment 385 was another raiding unit which operated in the Far East during 1945 carrying out deception raids, working with guerrillas, and gathering intelligence.

Royal Naval Commandos

The early amphibious raids by the Commandos pointed up an obvious need for better intelligence and control on the beaches. The earliest attempt at exerting some control on the beaches had been by the Royal Navy ratings manning the landing craft, but when this makeshift control proved inadequate, specialized 'beach parties' were organized and were first tried during OPERATION IRONCLAD on Madagascar. These specialized 'beach parties' proved so successful that the Royal Naval Commandos (sometimes known as 'Beachhead Commandos') were formed. Their duties included: landing in the first wave to clear the beaches, to mark limits of the beachhead, consolidate the beachhead, clearing personnel and equipment from the beachhead expeditiously, helping moor landing craft correctly, removing mines and underwater obstructions, taping the safe passage routes off the beaches, informing subsequent waves of important intelligence about the defenses and the beachhead, setting up ammunition and supply dumps, and act as a rearguard during withdrawal.

The first Royal Naval Commandos units were formed during the spring of 1942 with each Commando under the command of a Lieutenant Commander or a Commander. Each RN Commando had three sections, consisting of two officers (a beachmaster and assistant beachmaster), a petty officer, and seventeen other ratings. Later Royal Navy Commandos would consist of ten officers and sixty-six other ranks divided into three parties of twenty-five men each (one beachmaster, three assistant beachmasters, and twenty-two other ranks).

In August of 1942 members of the Royal Navy Commandos took part in the Dieppe raid, with a beach master and beach party assigned to each of the beaches. Some beach parties, however, could not reach their assigned beach due to heavy German fire. Members of the beach parties suffered very heavy casualties at Dieppe. Despite the problems at Dieppe, it was still obvious that the RN 'Beach Parties' were a necessity for any major amphibious operation and many of the smaller amphibious operations. It was also obvious that they needed specialized training and a school was established at Ardentinny, Scotland to train Royal Navy Commandos.

This school could accommodate 500 to 600 men and made good use of Loch Long for amphibious landing drills, reconnaissance, and gaining specialized beach skills. Other training included weapons usage, rock climbing, assault courses, embarkation and debarkation, using various types of landing craft under battle conditions, route marches, and field survival. Many of these skills were honed at Achnicarry where the RN Commandos were expected to pass the regular Commando training course and receive their green beret and F-S dagger. Some RN Commandos received additional training at Kabrit near the Suez Canal for duties in the Middle East, but Ardentinny was the main RN Commando training center. Experiences with landings in the Middle East proved valuable and along with the experience gained at Dieppe helped to mold and expand the Royal Navy Commando training program.

Once formed RN Commandos were assigned letters rather than numbers. By the end of 1943 twenty-two Royal Naval Commandos had been formed. During OPERATION TORCH on 8 November 1942, 410 RN Commandos proved themselves invaluable in the first major Anglo-American amphibious operation of the war. Four augmented RN Commandos — C, E, F, G, and parts of H and J — took part in the TORCH landings, which were carried out by three task forces (Western Task Force - Casablanca, Center Task Force - Oran, and the Eastern Task Force). The RN Commandos landed with the first assault elements and took charge of the beaches. After first eliminating snipers, they dug slit trenches on the beaches for protection and set up Lewis guns for use against low flying aircraft. The RN Commando's major task was to guide ashore 29,000 troops, 2400 vehicles, and 14,000 tons of supplies on three different beaches. Those RN Commandos working with American assault troops wore American uniforms since French troops were 'suspicious' of the British after the attack on the French fleet at Oran. Overall, the RN Commandos worked very efficiently during TORCH despite the fact that controlling the incoming landing craft proved very difficult. It was far better than it would have been had the RN Commandos not been present.

The next major operation for the RN Commandos was the invasion of Sicily which involved more than 2,000 ships and landing craft. Even though the RN Commandos were only involved with the Eastern Task Force (the British) during the invasion of Sicily, they still had to cover twenty-seven landing beaches. Once the assault troops were ashore the RN Commandos' job was often just getting started since they usually had to work the beaches for weeks directing in supplies and reinforcements.

In September of 1943 RN Commandos went in with the Army assault troops and Royal Marine Commandos when the allies landed in Italy. Later, during the advance up the Italian coast RN Commandos helped open up anchorages. At both the Salerno and Anzio landings RN Commandos found themselves forced to deal with mine fields before they could signal in the landing craft. At Anzio the RN Commandos had to use their F-S daggers to probe for wood-encased mines which could not be detected by metal detectors. Sandbars offshore also created great difficulty during the Anzio landings. RN Commandos performed admirably, keeping the beachhead functioning throughout the initial landings and for months afterward despite the almost constant German shelling.

H Royal Naval Commando served in Southeast Asia, receiving specialized training at the Jungle Battle School at Chittagong prior to going into combat during the landings on the Arakan coast. These operations commenced with SCREWDRIVER in February of 1944, followed by SCREWDRIVER II.

The largest RN Commando operation of the war was NEPTUNE, the naval portion of OVERLORD. Eight RN Commandos (F, J, L, P, Q, R, S, T) were scheduled and trained for this, the largest amphibious operation of the war. RN Commandos went in with the first wave in order to immediately judge whether landing craft of subsequent waves could land at the same point or had to go in elsewhere. RN Commandos took heavy casualties at Normandy, on some beaches having to dig in and fight off counterattacks, but their commando training made them effective at dealing with the Germans, a task they actually found less difficult than dealing with the congestion on the beaches. Wrecked landing craft and vehicles cluttering the beaches were a major problem, especially when they blocked the exits from the beachhead. Despite great difficulties RN Commandos managed to clear the obstacles, organize the exits, and began bringing supplies ashore. Most of the RN Commandos on the Normandy beaches stayed for at least 6 weeks helping to salvage sunken landing craft, moor Mulberry harbors and Phoenix piers, but most of all helping to bring order out of the chaos of the largest amphibious operation in the history of warfare.

The Normandy Invasion was the high point of RN Commando operations, but it did not mark the end of hostilities for the RN Commandos. RN Commandos took part in the capture of Walcheren and in crossing the Rhine at Arnhem (although not in the abortive airborne assault at Arnhem). Later, RN Commandos were sent to the Pacific to take part in the invasion of the Japanese home islands which fortunately did not prove necessary.

Not only did the Royal Navy Commandos have to go through the same rigorous training that Army and Marine Commandos went through but also had to perform a very difficult command and control task amidst the chaotic conditions of an amphibious operation. At the end of World War II the RN Commandos ceased to exist, but they left a proud tradition.

Combined Operations Assault Pilotage Parties (COPPs)

It quickly became obvious during early amphibious raids that more detailed information about the beaches to be assaulted was a necessity. As a result Royal Navy Lt Commander Nigel Clogstoun-Wilmott, an avid swimmer, developed the idea of using swimmers launched from submarines to carry out detailed beach reconnaissance prior to landings. In company with chanelist Roger Courtney, the founder of the Special Boat Service, Willmott, planned a reconnaissance of the beaches on the island of Rhodes. Since Willmott and Courtney were pioneering a new field, they had to develop makeshift waterproof equipment, primarily through the use of grease and prophylactics. Early in 1941 Willmott and Courtney carried out a reconnaissance of Rhodes. On the first night Clogstoun-Wilmott, the 'swimmer', spent three hours ashore while Courtney, the 'Rower', waited for him offshore in the canoe. Landings were made on each of the next successive four nights, gathering a great deal of useful information. Unfortunately the attack on Rhodes was cancelled, but Clogstoun-Wilmott's techniques had proven valid.

Clogstoun-Wilmott carried out reconnaissance of Kupho Island off the coast of Crete prior to the April raid by Royal Marines. During the summer of 1942 Clogstoun-Wilmott was asked to return to the UK to help prepare for the landings in North Africa. In September Clogstoun-Wilmott was given the go-ahead to form teams to carry out beach reconnaissance for OPERATION TORCH landings. During the year since his initial reconnaissance of the Rhodes beaches, Clogstoun-Wilmott had been working on improved equipment and techniques for beach surveying so his new teams would be better prepared for their missions.

Beginning with the TORCH landings Combined Operations Assault Pilotage Parties, or COPPs as it soon became known, assumed responsibility for marking beaches to guide in assault craft. After the TORCH landings fifty COPPs were proposed, but due to a shortage of navigators and other trained personnel, only ten could be formed before the end of the war. Normally, each of these parties consisted of eleven to twelve men.

In February of 1943, COPPs #3 and #4 carried out reconnaissance of Sicilian beaches prior to landings on the island, with #3 losing three men in the process. COPPS missions included locating enemy strongpoints, checking beach inclines, and gathering data necessary for landing troops and vehicles. Reconnaissance along the Sicilian coast was carried out in June of 1943 by #5 and #6 COPPs. #5 COPPS helped guide in the actual landings on 10 July 1943. #5 COPPS later went on to survey the beaches at Salerno prior to the allied landings on the Italian mainland.

By the fall of 1943 COPPs personnel were training to use X-craft midget subs for reconnaissance, although they found changing into their specialized swimming suits incredibly difficult in the cramped midget subs. During the winter of 1943/44, #1 and #2 COPPs made surveys of the Normandy beaches, primarily checking gradients and collecting soil samples. #1, #6, and #9 COPPs helped guide in the landings at Normandy in June of 1944. After taking part in the early Normandy reconnaissances #2 COPPs moved to the Mediterranean where they worked with the SBS and other raiders in the Aegean and Adriatic. #2 COPPs carried out the reconnaissance prior to the Lake Comacchio operation. After carrying out reconnaissance of the Anzio beaches #10 COPPs joined #2 COPPs in the Adriatic where they worked with the SBS and partisans prior to being deployed to India in 1945.

The first COPP deployed in the Far East was #7 which had gone out to India during the fall of 1943 and carried out reconnaissance of the Arakan along the Burmese coast. Serving in Asia along with COPPs were members of the Sea Reconnaissance Unit (SRU) which used paddle boards and breathing apparatus to carry out long distance infiltrations. SRU members were normally stronger swimmers than the members of COPPs. Both of these units, as part of Small Operations Group (SOG) were used to scout for good landing points for raiders.

By July of 1944, #3 and #4 COPPs were operating with SOG and making further reconnaissances of the Arakan. #8 COPPs was in Asia by early 1944 and was used for reconnaissance on Sumatra. Finally, in 1945 #1 and #9 COPPs were in Asia attached to SOG. It should be noted, however, that some of the COPP units which had served in Asia earlier had been rotated home by 1945.

Among the COPP operations in Europe were those prior to river crossings during the final drive into Germany. #5 COPPs, for example, carried out a difficult reconnaissance of minefields on the night of 23/24 March for the Rhine crossings, and in April of 1945, #7 COPPs carried out a reconnaissance for the Elbe River crossing.

STOWAGE CONTAINERS

A
spare clothes
2 fuse boxes
2 cups
Soap
4 escape boxes

B
Camouflage net
50-foot fishing line
Repair kit
Navigating gear
Paddle handgrip
Sounding reel
Flashlight
Grenade

C
Rations
Water cans

D
Magnetic holdfast
Grenade
Bailer and sponge
Paddle handgrip
Placing rod
4 limpet mines
Wrench
Spare clothes

E
Box of small gear
Matches
Stove
Placing rod
4 limpet mines
Spare clothes

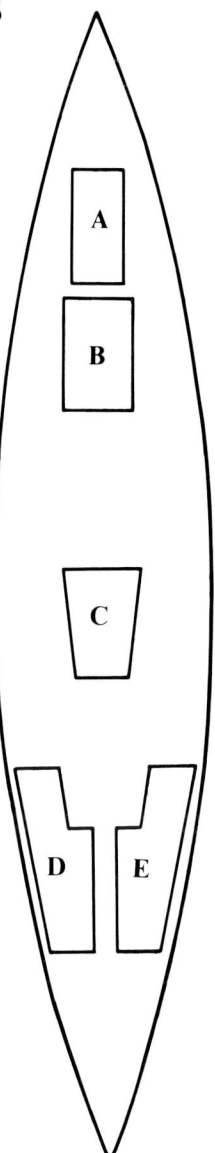

The COPPs Canoe was specifically designed for beach reconnaissance and sabatoge operations.

COMBAT TROOPS
in action

SS3001 Fallschirmjäger in Action (SC) . $5.95
WW II German paratroopers from training through the Normandy invasion. 84 photos, 17 detail drawings, 16 full color paintings, 50 pages.

SS3005 Panzergrenadiers in Action (SC) $5.95
WW II German armored assault infantry, their weapons, uniforms, tactics and the armored vehicles from which they fought. 100 photos, 28 detail drawings, 15 full color paintings, 50 pages.

SS3002 German Infantry in Action (SC) $5.95
The Wehrmacht sweeping through Europe and North Africa during WW II. 99 photos, 28 detail drawings, 14 full-color paintings, 50 pages.

SS3006 US Infantry-Vietnam (SC) $5.95
These mostly 18 and 19 year old draftees who were proud to be called 'Grunts' slugged it out in a vicious no-quarter guerrilla war waged in the hot steamy jungles of Vietnam. 108 photos, 51 detail drawings, 4 maps, 14 full color paintings, 50 pages.

SS3003 Waffen SS in Action (SC) $5.95
Germany's dreaded SS turned loose on Europe knowing only to attack. 98 photos, 22 detail drawings, 15 full-color paintings, 50 pages.

SS3007 US Elite Forces-Vietnam (SC) . $5.95
The US Army's Special Forces, Rangers, and LRRPs, the Navy's SEALs, the Marine Corps' Recons, and the Air Force's Combat Control Teams and Combat Security Police, their training and missions made them Elite troops. 102 photos, 28 detail drawings, 18 full-color paintings, 50 pages.